THE
BEATLES
COMPANION

George, John, Ringo, and Paul at London Airport in early 1965.

THE BEATLES COMPANION

THE FAB FOUR IN FILM, PERFORMANCE, RECORDING, AND PRINT

Ted Greenwald

SMITHMARK

A FRIEDMAN GROUP BOOK

This edition published in 1992
by SMITHMARK Publishers Inc.
112 Madison Avenue
New York, New York 10016

ISBN 0-8317-0717-8

THE BEATLES COMPANION
The Fab Four in Film, Performance, Recording, and Print
was prepared and produced by
Michael Friedman Publishing Group, Inc.
15 West 26th Street
New York, NY 10010

Editor: Elizabeth Viscott Sullivan
Art Director: Jeff Batzli
Designer: Robert W. Kosturko
Layout: Tanya Ross Hughes
Photography Editor: Christopher C. Bain

Typeset by Bookworks Plus
Color separations by Scantrans
Printed and bound in Hong Kong by Leefung Asco Ltd.

SMITHMARK Books are available for bulk purchase for sales
promotions and premium use. For details write or telephone the
Manager of Special Sales, SMITHMARK Publishers Inc., 112 Madison
Avenue, New York, New York 10016. (212) 532-6600.

Dedication

To John, Paul, George, and Ringo, for returning, bodhisattvalike, to live as mortal men.

Acknowledgements

The author gratefully acknowledges his debt to Harry Castleman and Walter Podrazik, Bill Harry, L.R.E. King, Jeffrey Levy, Mark Lewisohn, Peter McCabe and Robert D. Schonfeld, Philip Norman, Charles Reinhart, Tom Schultheiss, Carol D. Terry, Allen J. Weiner, and others who gathered the timbers from which his words were built. Special thanks to L.R.E. King for checking the accuracy of the manuscript.

Contents

In the ring in early 1964 with heavyweight contender Cassius Clay, later known as Muhammad Ali.

Introduction

P A G E   8

C H A P T E R   O N E

The Beatles: A Brief History

P A G E   1 0

CHAPTER TWO
Beatle Biographies and Beatle People
PAGE 14

CHAPTER THREE
The Beatles on Record
PAGE 42

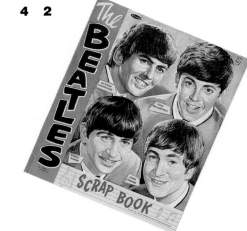

CHAPTER FOUR
The Beatles on Stage:
Major Concert Appearances
PAGE 90

CHAPTER FIVE
The Beatles on Film
PAGE 102

CHAPTER SIX
The Beatles in Print:
A Selected Bibliography
PAGE 110

Index
PAGE 118

Introduction

During the late 1950s, Britain was overrun by musically untrained teenaged boys who played the anglicized African-American hybrid known as skiffle. Even so, at the time it was well beyond imagining that four of them would abandon skiffle for the cruder, more subversive rock-'n'roll; discover each other and become fast friends; pursue fortunes that they dared to propose might make them "bigger than Elvis"; withstand the incessant grinding of the star-making machinery; and finally, change the face of music—not popular music, not the music of their era, but the entire long, grand tradition of music itself.

One reason for the Beatles' endurance is the sheer volume of material and artifacts that John, Paul, George, and Ringo have left in their wake. Scholars of medieval music affirm that the composers of the Middle Ages who are recognized today are those who managed to distribute their scores most widely throughout Europe. Likewise, the Beatles spread their products far and wide. For nearly a decade they virtually monopolized the popular arts, generating not only recordings, but books, newsprint, photographs, films, and miscellaneous objets d'art, either directly through their own ingenuity or by inspiring others to create as well. Today, over twenty years after the group's demise, their presence continues to reverberate through the airwaves, across the pages of the popular press, and through the music we hear and the images we see every day.

Nonetheless, *The Beatles Companion* is not about the Beatles' music, but about people and events behind it, and the artifacts the band left in their wake. This book is for listeners who have been moved by the Beatles' music and want to know more about who they were and what they did; the casual fan who wants to find out what other things the Beatles were doing when his or her favorite song was a hit; and the weekend Beatlemaniac who owns a VCR and wants to know what he or she might rent for an evening's entertainment. Likewise, this book is for the neophyte collector, who will find the lists of films, videos, and concert appearances helpful in sorting out the vast archive of video and audio material available among tape traders, and the survey of acetates useful introductions to these areas.

In order to make even the most obscure references as accessible as possible, the text is studded with record company catalog numbers and release dates. Recordings issued on CD in either the U.S., the U.K., or both are noted by the letters "CD" before the catalog number. The date, when given in parentheses, is that of the original vinyl release. Catalog numbers for recordings unavailable as CDs are prefaced by the tags "US," denoting a United States release, or "UK," denoting a British release. Wherever possible, the U.S. catalog number is used. If you see an entry marked "UK," the record hasn't been released in the U.S.

Another more important reason why the Beatles have such tenacity, of course, is the special quality of their music. Inspired by rhythm & blues and rock'n'roll records imported from America, they recognized the vinyl disk as their primary medium and nurtured it to unparalleled heights of cultural influence. *Sgt. Pepper's Lonely Hearts Club Band* did for popular music what the evolution of large symphonic forms did for the European classical tradition, as it demonstrated a palette of sound so broad and subtle that it could bear the most ambitious or fanciful artistic aims.

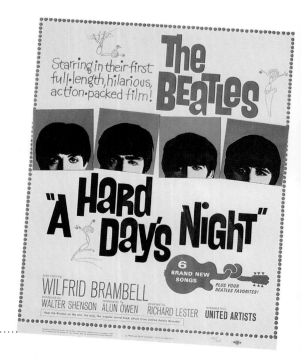

A visit to Madame Tussaud's waxworks in 1964. The Fabs' wax likenesses appear on the cover of *Sgt. Pepper's Lonely Hearts Club Band.*

The Contents of *The Beatles Companion*

The sheer volume of Beatle-related material makes it reasonable to limit the scope of a book of this sort. *The Beatles Companion,* therefore, covers matters relating to John, Paul, George, and Ringo as a group, rather than as individuals. Their individual careers, both during and after the Beatles, are mentioned wherever appropriate, but this volume makes no attempt to cover them fully.

It should also be pointed out that, despite the years of intense scrutiny focused upon the Fab Four, Beatle scholarship is an evolving field. Even aside from the incredible volume of Beatle news to be sifted through and documented, new information is being generated, and old information discarded, at a great pace. Many "facts" that have been passed on from one book to another are found to be, rather, misconceptions. Such errors will only be rectified by dogged primary-source research of a kind few authors are willing to take on, and much work remains to be done. No doubt, some of these nonfacts have found their way into the pages of this book. I trust (and hope), however, that they are few and far between, or at least that they leave the outline of the truth intact.

In any case, it is an overwhelming experience simply to ponder the breadth of creative output achieved in less than a decade by four provincial British kids who suddenly found themselves at, in John's phrase, "the toppermost of the poppermost."

The Beatles: A Brief History

John formed his first band, the Quarry Men, as a lark when he was in high school in 1957. Around the same time, Paul dragged his brother onto a Butlin's Holiday Camp stage because he couldn't resist the opportunity to sing. George joined the Rebels in order to emulate his hero, Carl Perkins, and Ringo played drums for a living because that was all he knew how to do. Individually, they were monomaniacally determined to play rock'n'roll, and when the four of them finally found each other, the combination was magical. As John would recall, "What we generated was fantastic when we played straight rock, and there was no one to touch us in Britain."

The Beatles were part of a Liverpool phenomenon the press tagged "Merseybeat," a grassroots flowering of musical organizations similar to those of San Francisco in 1966, and of London a decade later. Merseybeat began in 1956 with a British singer named Lonnie Donegan, who adapted the African-derived blues of such American singers as Leadbelly for British consumption, evolving a style called skiffle. Skiffle's distinguishing features were a simple but infectious rhythm and an ensemble that featured acoustic guitar, washboard percussion, and tea-chest bass (a string attached to a wooden shipping crate pulled taut by a broomstick). The skiffle fad swept across Britain, paving the way for the arrival of rock'n'roll two years later and leaving in its wake scores of teenagers inspired by the possibility of overnight stardom.

The Quarry Men were one of the more enduring skiffle outfits. Under John's leadership, the group steadily upgraded its roster, adding Paul McCartney, then fifteen years old, on guitar and piano in late 1957. The following year, guitarist George Harrison, one year Paul's junior, was invited to join. By 1959, through a combination of choice and attrition, John, Paul, and George were the group's only steady members. Opportunities to perform were scarce, but they continued to play,

sometimes as a trio but usually with one of several occasional drummers. (Drum kits were expensive, and few schoolboys could afford one.)

A friend of John's from the Liverpool Art College, bass player Stu Sutcliffe, became a steady member in early 1960, and the band went through a series of name changes. Finally, they settled on the Silver Beatles, a double-entendre incorporating references to both beat music and Buddy Holly's Crickets. ("Silver" was retained to blunt the effect of such an odd-sounding name.)

During the early years, the Beatles were not regarded as the best of the Mersey bands. In fact, before their first trip to Hamburg in August 1960, for which they took on drummer Pete Best, they were known as one of the worst. It was only after their return that the denizens of Liverpool's clubs began to take notice; over a hundred nights of eight-hour performances in the rough-and-tumble clubs of the Reeperbahn had honed the Silver Beatles' musical skills and showmanship to a fine edge.

John, Paul, George, and Pete returned from their second stint in Hamburg in the summer of 1961 without Stu, but with a record they had made backing singer Tony Sheridan, a hepped-up arrangement of "My Bonnie (Lies Over the Ocean)." When Brian Epstein, manager of the Liverpool branch of Northern England Music Stores (NEMS), began getting requests for the record, he decided to step around the block to the Cavern Club to see what all the fuss was about. Epstein didn't know anything about rock'n'roll, but he felt overwhelmed by the Beatles. He was convinced that if he dressed them in suits and taught them to take proper bows after each song, the rest of the world would feel that way, too.

For six months, Epstein tried to interest one record company after another in his boys. Every time, he was rejected. A deal with Decca records, for whom the Beatles recorded an audition on New Year's Day, 1962, slipped through his fingers.

Finally, in April, a chance meeting with a music publisher earned him an audience with George Martin, then a producer of oddball comedy records with EMI's backwater label, Parlophone. Martin was impressed not by the Beatles' music, but by their personalities. He offered them a recording contract.

In the years before they signed with Parlophone, the band had performed incessantly throughout the Merseyside area. Once they had a contract, they undertook a series of grueling national tours with newly recruited drummer Ringo Starr and, little by little, their records began to sell in Britain. They continued to tour throughout 1963, at the same time inundating the British radio and television airwaves with interviews, special performances, and publicity stunts. As 1964 began, Capitol Records agreed to distribute their recordings in the U.S., and waged a huge promotional campaign. By the time they appeared on *The Ed Sullivan Show* on February 9, success in America was a foregone conclusion.

Above: Fans relive Beatlemania in 1984 at the premier of Paul's film *Give My Regards to Broad Street.* Opposite, top and bottom: On *The Ed Sullivan Show*, February 1964.

I LOVE THE BEATLES

An enterprising fan attempts to crash the set of *A Hard Day's Night* in 1964.

With the American market firmly in hand, the Beatles' success spread across the world with a speed and intensity so fierce that there seemed to be nothing they couldn't achieve. Their wit impressed the pundits, their charm won over the skeptics, and their music made people listen who had never considered popular music worthy of their attention. Each new record topped the charts, and critics agreed that it was better than the last. By 1965 their concerts, invariably sold out, were no longer held in cinemas and concert halls, but in sports arenas, where writhing masses of teenagers gathered to shriek in ecstasy as the Beatles, inaudible, played behind rows of police officers. Their movies, first *A Hard Day's Night* and *Help!*,

and later *Yellow Submarine,* were inevitably hailed as innovations in entertainment.

But there was a downside to this phenomenal rise to fame. While the Beatles were on tour, they were confined to their hotel rooms, only to have fans climb up drainpipes to get into their windows. When they were in London, they were mobbed in the streets, and fans would sneak into their homes to steal their personal effects. Paternity suits mounted, and jealous boyfriends of female fans even took pot shots at them. Their every word was repeated, interpreted, misquoted, and often misunderstood. Reporters bombarded them with personal, insulting, or just plain stupid questions.

Everyone, it seemed, wanted a piece of the action: Fans expressed their adoration, businessmen sought their endorsement for products, and musicians imitated their haircuts. The Beatles found themselves at the center of a cynical bid for political support when British Prime Minister Harold Wilson, on October 26, 1965, awarded each Beatle the prestigious MBE (Member of the British Empire), an honor usually reserved for war heroes. The fans were delighted, the Beatles embarrassed; several prominent MBE-holders returned their medals in protest. What had begun as an adolescent whim, a chance to dress up in leather and sing favorite songs in front of a dancing, sweating crowd, had in many ways become a cage.

And the music was changing. It took on subtleties that couldn't be adequately represented before a stadium full of screaming children, stylistic features that didn't lend themselves to Top Ten radio, intentions that the Beatles themselves didn't quite understand. On August 29, 1966, they made their last official concert appearance and retired from the stage to concentrate on their recordings.

With the Beatles sequestered at Abbey Road Studios, the artistic growth that characterized their work in 1965's *Rubber Soul* continued at an accelerated pace. *Revolver* (1966) plumbed depths of emotional expression ("Eleanor Rigby") and technical expertise ("Tomorrow Never Knows") unprecedented in modern popular music. The landmark *Sgt. Pepper's Lonely Hearts Club Band* (1967), with its aural illusions, seamless segues, and extensive use of unusual instruments and sounds, represented a new pinnacle in the coloristic and imaginative aspects of recorded music.

With the sprawling White Album (1968), a new Beatles emerged, one completely unfettered by the expectations of the listening public. This impression, suggested by the eight-minute abstract sound collage "Revolution 9," was soon confirmed by solo projects such as John and Yoko's *Unfinished Music No. 1: Two Virgins* [US: Apple T-5001 (1968)] and George's *Electronic Sounds* [US: Zapple ST-3358 (1969)]. As those records also indicate, the individual Beatles were no longer content to submerge their personalities for the benefit of the whole. The Fabs, which John had once called "four parts of the same person," had begun to disintegrate.

The jet-set elite had introduced them to psychoactive drugs—marijuana via Bob Dylan in 1964, LSD via their dentist in early 1965—which they embraced as both an escape from, and a transcendence of, what they had become. Searching for a sense of purpose higher than that which they had achieved through their music, they became momentary disciples of the Maharishi Mehesh Yogi in 1967, which alienated them further

The Fab Four display their M.B.E. (Membership of the British Empire) awards in 1965.

Despite the optimism that surrounded the post-*Sgt. Pepper* era, the Beatles' artistic vision became increasingly less focused, their business affairs a tangle of greed and naiveté, and their personal affairs alarmingly complex. John's all-consuming relationship with his second wife Yoko Ono, and Paul's with his wife Linda Eastman, effectively ended the symbiosis between the principal Beatles. In addition, George had long since tired of being a Beatle, and was eager to move beyond the shadows of Lennon and McCartney. At the dawn of 1969, entering into what would become a seventeen-month effort to make the *Let It Be* album and film, the Fab Four found themselves unwilling to continue to fulfill the role of the world's most celebrated entertainers. By the end of 1970, Paul McCartney found it necessary to sue his partners in order to avoid having his affairs managed by Klein, the man chosen by the other three Beatles.

With the legal and personal dissolution of their partnership, John, Paul, George, and Ringo left what remained of the Beatles to be picked clean by lawyers, accountants, record companies, and the popular press. In the decades since, their popularity has shown no sign of fading, and rereleases of their hits periodically rise to the top of the charts. Hopes of a reunion, fed by small-scale collaborations on Ringo's occasional solo albums, were dashed by John's tragic death in December 1980. Nonetheless, 1990 found both Paul and Ringo performing Beatle songs onstage once again (albeit not together), and the recent reactivation of George's career revives perennial hopes that the three remaining Beatles might one day make music together again.

from the mainstream audience. Brian Epstein, who had struggled to keep the Fab Four out of controversy, now watched in resignation as his boys grew facial hair, admitted to dropping acid, and announced their opposition to U.S. involvement in Vietnam. As the group spent more time involved in esoteric pursuits and less in maintaining their public image, Epstein's life, once dedicated to the Fab Four, became increasingly insular and chaotic. On August 17, 1967, he died of an accidental overdose of barbiturates.

Epstein's death was the beginning of the end of the Beatles. They never recovered from the loss of the man whose faith and vision had been the driving force behind their fame. Bravely, perhaps foolishly, they decided to manage themselves. When their first independent movie, the self-produced and -directed TV film *Magical Mystery Tour,* proved frivolous and self-indulgent, it became evident—for the first time—that the Beatles weren't infallible.

Finding their earnings subject to a 90-percent tax rate, the Beatles decided to invest their income in an entertainment conglomerate which they named Apple Corps Ltd. The company, which Paul dubbed an exercise in "Western communism" on the May 15, 1968 broadcast of *The Tonight Show,* was their statement to the mainstream world about the proper relationship between art and commerce; Apple was a place where artists of all styles and media could present and obtain finances for their ideas. The Beatles signed a stable of old friends and young up-and-comers to Apple Records, bought scripts for Apple Films, opened an Apple Boutique, and solicited projects in newspaper advertisements. After a short time, however, the organization was overrun with charlatans and hangers-on. In desperation, the Beatles hired the Rolling Stones' former manager, Allen Klein, to pare down Apple's operations and personnel to bare essentials.

The Beatles during the recording of *Let It Be* in the Apple Recording Studio, January 1969.

Beatle Biographies and Beatle People

John Lennon

From the moment he first heard the stuttering chorus of Elvis Presley's "Heartbreak Hotel" in 1956, John Lennon was destined to become a rock'n'roll star. That he also became, along with his partner and competitor Paul McCartney, one of the most influential songwriters of our time was the result of a mysterious blending of his own innate talent and the zeitgeist of his generation.

The quest for stardom, which began with attention-getting pranks well before he entered high school, appears to have been a legacy of John's home life. Shortly after his birth on October 9, 1940, his mother Julia, a strong-willed and fun-loving woman, placed him in the care of his stern but equally strong-willed Aunt Mimi. Soon thereafter, his father went off to sea under unknown circumstances that kept him away for several years. When he finally returned, John, at age five, was asked to choose between mother and father. Although he asked to remain with Julia, he found himself, once again, in Mimi's care.

An intelligent and quick-witted child, John became a notorious troublemaker at school, throwing blackboards out of windows and bullying his fellow students. In his teens he discovered that his mother, who was living only a short distance away, shared his interests in music and mischief, and they became allies against Aunt Mimi's efforts to control his behavior. When John was seventeen, however, John lost Julia again, this time permanently, when she died in a car accident. Many years later, John recognized that his lack of a sense of being loved as a child formed the foundation of his compulsion to be publicly adored. It was also the source of occasional explosions of rage that, throughout the 1960s, were kept hidden by the Beatles' management.

If the Beatles began as John's surrogate for parental affection, by 1965 they had come to represent all that was false in the world. Audiences screamed themselves hoarse whether the band played well or poorly. Such embarrassments as paternity suits and episodes of violence, particularly his beating of Liverpool DJ Bob Wooler at Paul's twenty-first birthday party, were buried beneath large sums of hush money. Mothers brought their crippled children before the Fab Four to be healed. When John responded by trying to deliver a more honest image of himself ("I'm a Loser," December 1964), he was asked in no uncertain terms to act more like a cuddly teddy-bear pop star. Over the latter half of the 1960s, he escaped into drugs, musical experimentation, spiritual quests, and finally into his relationship with avant-garde artist Yoko Ono.

Yoko, whom John first met in 1966, reawakened his sense of adventure. Early on, with songs such as "A Hard Day's Night" (1964) and "Help!" (1965), he had proven himself capable of churning out hits in the manner that had long been Paul's raison d'être. Later experiments had left him with a feeling that, despite the sophistication of "Tomorrow Never Knows" (1966) or "I Am the Walrus" (1967), Gene Vincent's "Be-Bop-A-Lula" (Vincent-Davis) communicated in a more elemental manner. Under Yoko's influence, he was able to abandon his preconceptions about the nature of music, producing the cacophony of the "Revolution 9" (1968), the gentleness of "Because" (1969), or the directness of "I Want You (She's So Heavy)" (1969).

With the breakup of the Beatles in 1969, John was flooded with feelings of both intense bitterness and exhilarating freedom. A series of collaborative films, records, and exhibitions with Yoko tested the boundaries of art and the patience of fans. In order to debunk the Beatles mythology, he gave vitriolic interviews in which he seemed to take great pleasure in heaping abuse upon Paul. He used his newfound independence to work toward ends that he felt were better justified than

record company profits, including U.S. withdrawal from Vietnam, the freeing of political prisoners, and equality for women.

By the mid-1970s, though, his musical output had become sporadic. January 1975 marked the beginning of a five-year retirement from music during which he devoted himself to raising his newborn son Sean. The experience, for the first time, of a close-knit family appears to have given John the most happy and rewarding years of his life, and he returned to the public spotlight in 1980 in his most optimistic mood ever. His record of that year, *Double Fantasy* [CD: Geffen 2002-1], sold more than 7 million copies and remained at Number One for eight weeks, making it the most commercially successful record of his post-Beatles career.

This new phase of John Lennon's life was cut tragically short on December 12, 1980, when he was killed by a madman's bullet.

Above: John and Yoko's "bed-in" for peace at the Amsterdam Hilton, March 1969. Opposite, top: John surrounded by fans, August 1966. Opposite, bottom: John during the filming of the BBC series *Not Only But Also*, November 1966.

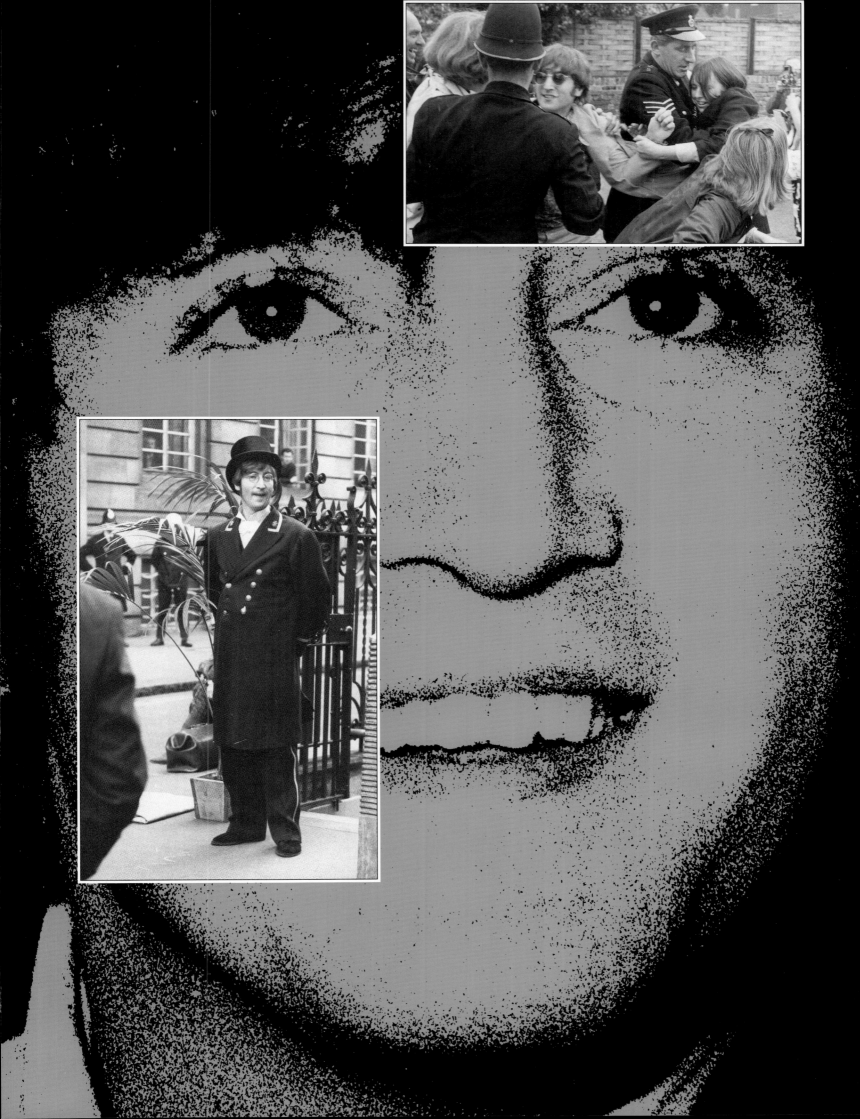

I was never really a street kid or a tough guy. . . . But it was a big part of one's life to look tough. I spent the whole of my childhood with shoulders up around the top of me head and me glasses off, because glasses were sissy, and walking in complete fear, but with the toughest-looking little face you've ever seen. I'd get into trouble just because of the way I looked; I wanted to be this tough James Dean all the time. It took a lot of wrestling to stop doing that.

—*Rolling Stone*, December 5, 1980, reprinted in *The Ballad of John and Yoko*, Jonathan Cott and Christine Doudna, eds., 1982

We had these people thrust on us. Like being insulted by these junked-up middle-class bitches and bastards who would be commenting on our working-classness and our manners. . . . It was a fuckin' humiliation. One has to completely humiliate oneself to be what the Beatles were, and that's what I resent. It just happens bit by bit, until this complete craziness surrounds you and you're doing exactly what you don't want to do with people you can't stand—the people you hated when you were ten.

—*Rolling Stone*, January 7/February 4, 1971, reprinted in *The Ballad of John and Yoko*, Jonathan Cott and Christine Doudna, eds., 1982

Newspaper people have a habit of putting you on the front page to sell their papers, and then after they've sold their papers and got big circulations, they say, "Look what we've done for you."

—*John Lennon: For the Record*, Peter McCabe and Robert D. Schonfeld, 1984

John in 1965.

On the *Magical Mystery Tour* bus, September 1967.

John (circa 1965).

Some people thought we'd sold out by leaving Liverpool or leaving even one particular club—the Cavern....If you left one dance hall to play at another, you lost a few people. And so when we left Liverpool we lost a few but gained a lot more. And when we left London and England—we lost a few in England because they thought we'd sold out to America.

—*Rolling Stone*, June 28, 1970, reprinted in *The Ballad of John and Yoko*, Jonathan Cott and Christine Doudna, eds., 1982

When we hit town, we hit it, we were not pissing about. You know, there's photographs of me groveling about, crawling about in Amsterdam on my knees, coming out of whorehouses and things like that....And the police escorted me to the places because they never wanted a big scandal....Everybody wants the image to carry on. The press around with you want you to carry on because they want the free drinks and the free whores and the fun. Everybody wants to keep on the band-wagon....Who was going to knock us when there's a million pounds to be made?

—*Rolling Stone*, January 7/February 4, 1971, reprinted in *The Ballad of John and Yoko*, Jonathan Cott and Christine Doudna, eds., 1982

It's pretty hard when you are Caesar and everyone is saying how wonderful you are and they are giving you all the goodies and the girls, it's pretty hard to break out of that, to say "Well, I don't want to be king. I want to be real."

—*Red Mole* magazine, March 8–22, 1971, reprinted in *The Lennon Companion*, Elizabeth Thompson and David Gutman, eds., 1988

Paul McCartney

Pegged instantly in the public imagination as "the cute one," Paul McCartney has always been adept at retreating behind a barrier of affability and personal magnetism, making it difficult to evaluate the more subtle aspects of his personality. At school, he was both savvy and intelligent enough to glide by with minimal effort and a healthy dollop of charm. In later years, these traits were reflected in his uncanny ability to create pop-music masterpieces such as "Penny Lane" and "Hey Jude," in which heartfelt sincerity is wedded with a palpable sense of detachment.

Born on June 18, 1942, Paul grew up in a humble, but supportive, family environment. His father, a cotton salesman, had led a band during the 1920s, and taught Paul how to play jazz standards on the piano. He took trumpet lessons as a child and, after attending a Lonnie Donegan concert in 1956, began to teach himself how to play the guitar. With the discovery that, although right-handed for every other purpose, he was a left-handed guitar player, Paul's fate was sealed: His guitar, restrung to be played upside-down, became a consuming passion. The same year, his mother died of cancer, leaving him to learn hard lessons in discipline and self-reliance.

Paul's neutral public stance, belied by a private inner resolve, became a keystone to the Beatles' internal politics. Unlike John and George, he was not a natural troublemaker. He was agreeable to the most mischievous activities, however, and adapted himself to the personalities of the others. With John, he shared the loss of his mother (and his subsequent drive for public acceptance). With George, he shared a commitment to the technical aspects of musical excellence. After Stuart Sutcliffe left the group in 1961, it was Paul who gave up his instruments, guitar and piano, for the bass when nobody else in the band was willing or able to do so—and went on to become one of the most influential and inventive players of the instrument.

Although John was the acknowledged leader of the Beatles, Paul took the reins after Brian Epstein's death in 1967, and led the other three into such projects as *Sgt. Pepper's Lonely Hearts Club Band* (widely hailed as their most ambitious and most influential album), the *Magical Mystery Tour* film and soundtrack, and the *Let It Be* album and documentary film project. He took on more responsibility for the band's productivity as the others lapsed into an apathy borne of having conquered the world several times over. By the summer of 1968, when the Beatles were recording what was to become known as the White Album, John, Paul, and George were each diverging from the musical formulas that the group had pioneered together. The songs became less and less collaborative efforts and more the songs of each Beatle, with the other three Beatles serving as backing musicians.

It is clear that for Paul—in stark contrast to John and George—being a Beatle was enough. He had thrived on the extroversion, publicity, and adulation of the mid-1960s, and came to miss those things as the others insulated themselves from the excesses of Beatlemania. His efforts to revive the spirit of the group in 1969, which included plans for a comeback tour, a television special, and a feature film, ultimately galvanized the differences between them.

Although Paul had tried the hardest to keep the band together, it was also he who took the most decisive step toward ending the group. In 1970, rather than accept the decision of the others to hand over the control of their careers to Allen Klein, he initiated court action to dissolve the Beatles' partnership.

In the years since the breakup, Paul has been the most active and commercially successful of the four ex-Beatles. Soon after leaving the Beatles, he formed Wings, which over the course of eight albums propelled him to the heights of pop stardom all over again, most notably with the smashing success of the *Band on the Run* album [CD: Capitol CDP 7 46675 2 (1987)]. *Guinness Book of World Records* has dubbed him "the most successful songwriter of all time," as he composed forty-three songs that sold over a million copies between 1962 and 1978.

His most recent solo effort, *Flowers in the Dirt* [CD: Capitol C291653 (1989)], has been hailed as his best in years; catchy and contemporary, yet durable upon repeated listenings. Several of the songs on this album were collaborations between Paul and singer/songwriter Elvis Costello.

Upon *Flowers in the Dirt*'s release, Paul assembled a new band and embarked upon a remarkable worldwide tour. Spotlighting a larger number of Beatle songs than ever before, his 1989–90 shows were characterized by sold-out performances and enthusiastic reviews. On June 30, 1990, he and the band performed at the star-studded Knebworth charity music festival in Hertfordshire, England. His rendition of "Hey Jude" from that show appears on *Knebworth* [CD: Polydor 847 042 2 (1990)].

Given his 1991 collaboration with American conductor Carl Davis on a symphony for the Royal Liverpool Philharmonic Orchestra's 150th anniversary, Paul McCartney appears likely to remain an active musical force well into the next century.

Above: Paul as a student at the Liverpool Institute Grammar School. Opposite, top: Paul and an Austrian fan have a drink in the village of Obertauern, where the Fab Four filmed a portion of *Help!* in 1965. Opposite, bottom: Paul at the Apple Recording Studios during the *Get Back* sessions, 1969.

[We] got a little bit blasé about civic honours after a while, because you sort of realize, "Well, what is it, freedom of a city? What can you do? What does this mean? Can you rob banks?" . . . You get the key to Indianapolis. It's all a big ceremony, really. Picture with the Lord Mayor. And meet his daughters. And you used to have to do something to keep yourself amused because it was so mind-numbingly boring. . . . I used to fake a little squint just to keep myself amused. The others used to like it if they'd spot it. It's great. You expect them to go away saying, "You get close up and he's got a funny thing with his eye."

—*The Paul McCartney World Tour,* Paul Du Noyer, ed., 1989

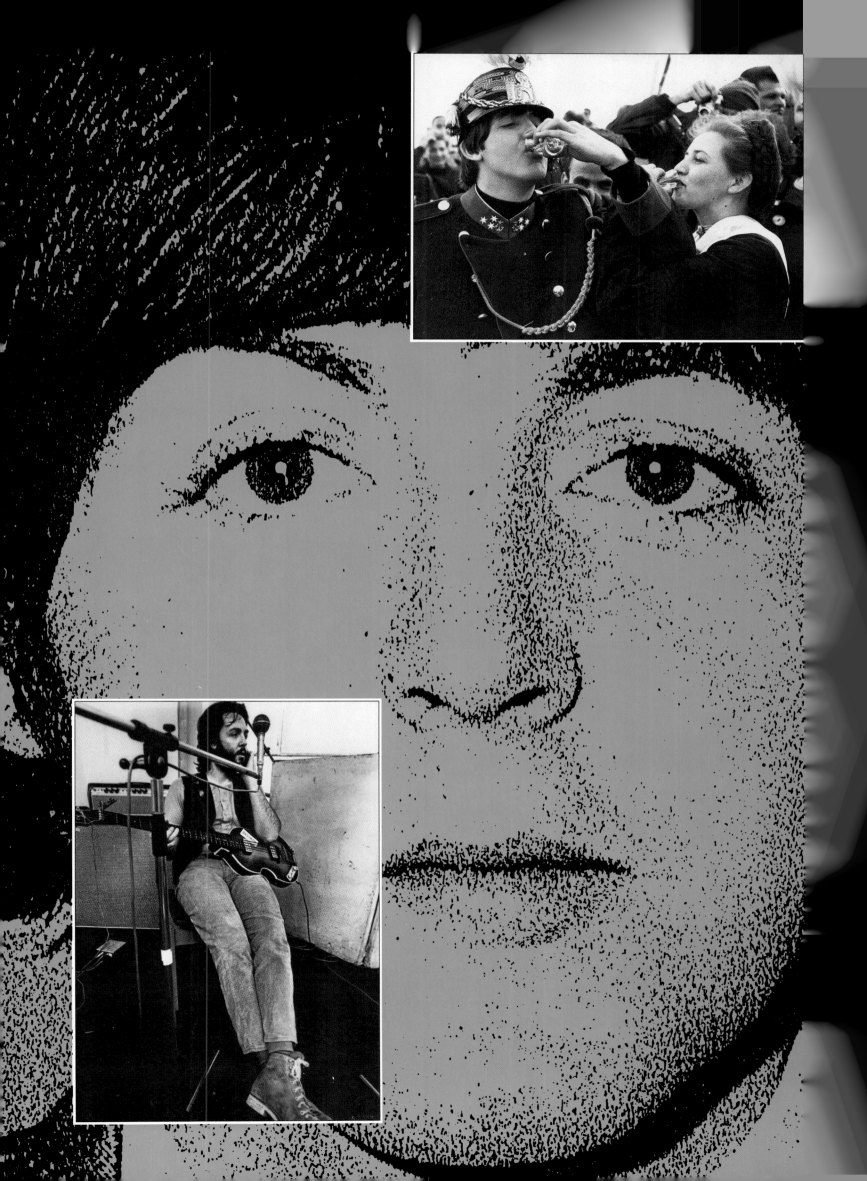

Below: Paul making his way into the barbed-wire-protected Futurist Theatre, Scarborough, England, 1964. Right: Paul in 1964.

I had a very rich avant-garde period, which was such a buzz, making movies and stuff. I was living on my own in London, and all the other guys were married in the suburbs. They were very square in my mind, and they'd come in, and come into my pad where there'd be people all hanging out and weird sculptures and stuff, and I'd be piecing together little films and stuff. I remember John came and was quite turned on by it all. When he made the album Two Virgins, he was hopeless, technically. I had to set up a couple of tape recorders and show him this whole system that I used, and he, being John—the difference between him and me, he'd make the record of it. Whereas, being me, I'd do it and experiment with it and then bring it to our mainstream records.

—*The Paul McCartney World Tour*, Paul Du Noyer, ed., 1989

We never got much real craziness. The worst of the craziness was in Paris once, someone pulled out a pair of scissors and tried to cut your hair off, and you know what people are like about their haircut. . . . But the hysteria was kind of benevolent hysteria. So it was really kind of nice. It was just, like, applause, and once or twice it was dead handy, because if you're out of tune or not singing too good, it didn't matter.

—*The Paul McCartney World Tour*, Paul Du Noyer, ed., 1989

Someone from the office rang me up and said, "Look, Paul, you're dead." And I said, "Oh, I don't agree with that." And they said, "Look, what are you going to do about it? It's a big thing breaking in America. You're dead." And so I said, "Leave it, just let them say it. It'll probably be the best publicity we've ever had, and I won't have to do a thing except stay alive...." Coincidentally, around about that time, I was playing down a lot of the old Beatle image and getting a bit more to what I felt was me, letting me beard grow and not being so hung up on keeping fresh and clean. I looked different, more laid back, so I had people coming up saying, "You're not him!" And I was beginning to think, "I am, you know, but I know what you mean. I don't look like him, but believe me."

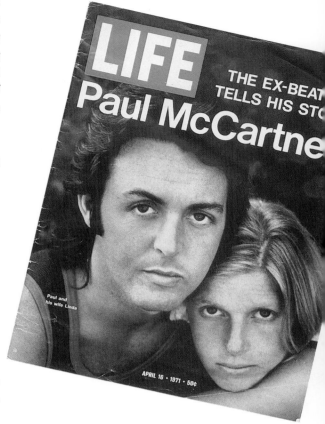

—*Paul McCartney in His Own Words* by Paul Gambaccini, 1973

With two guitarists, with John and George, it was always John saying, "Put that up a bit" and then George would come in and he'd put his up a bit, then George Martin would be saying "Can you turn the amps down, please?" And John would look at George and say, "How much are you going down? Let's go down to five, all right?" John'd go down to six. "OK, I'm at five!" "You Bugger, you're not! You're at six!" There was always this terrible rivalry!

—*The Beatles: Recording Sessions* by Mark Lewisohn, 1988

If the Beatles ever wanted a sound, it was R&B. That's what we used to listen to, what we used to like and what we wanted to be like. Black, that was basically it. Arthur Alexander.

—*The Beatles: Recording Sessions* by Mark Lewisohn, 1988

Recording Paul's composition "Thingumybob" with the Black Dyke Mills brass band in Bradford, Yorkshire, June 1968. Martha, Paul's sheepdog, stands at his side.

George Harrison

As a child, George Harrison rode to school in a pale green Liverpool Corporation bus driven by his father. Like Paul McCartney, who rode the same bus, he came from a stable working-class family. Born on February 25, 1943, George was the youngest of four children.

From the start, George displayed an independent, solitary demeanor, which made it all the more difficult to handle him as, during late childhood, he began to do poorly in school. Unlike the boisterous John Lennon, George was a silent rebel; he expressed his alienation by appropriating meticulously the tough-guy fashions of Liverpool's teen outcasts, the Teddy Boys. Having noticed sketches of guitars penciled into his school books, George's mother bought one for him when he was thirteen years old. With her encouragement, he taught himself to play from a book.

One year later, in early 1958, George's schoolmate Paul let him tag along to a rehearsal of the Quarry Men. John, nearly three years his senior, regarded him as a pest, but tolerated him in deference to his partner. Nonetheless George, having virtually flunked out of school, doggedly followed the band until they allowed him to sit in onstage. By the end of the year, he became an official member.

Unlike Paul and John, playing the guitar did not come easily to George. But the struggle made him apply himself all the more rigorously, and eventually he came to match the others in skill. One suspects that George became the Beatles' lead guitarist, usually a center-stage role, primarily because John wasn't interested in learning the licks. In recorded rehearsals even as late as 1964, his inability to improvise a solo is painfully evident. However, George left the Beatles a top-notch lead guitarist, whom even such a revered authority as Eric Clapton regarded as one of the best. The great forbearance required to improve so dramatically is one of the essential characteristics of the Beatle known for so long as "the quiet one," and then as the one who wouldn't stop preaching about his religious convictions.

George's forbearance is also evident with respect to his position in the Beatle hierarchy. By the time the Fab Four began to attract public attention in late 1963, his talent was fully eclipsed by the collaboration of, and competition between, John and Paul. That had not always been the case, however. George's presence on the January 1,

1962 Decca audition tape—he sang the lead on five out of the twelve songs not written by John and Paul—was far more prominent than it would be just a short time later. At some point, it appears, he was nudged into the background, where he remained until well into the group's career.

George emerged as a musical force in the group with 1966's *Revolver*, the first Beatles album to manifest his fascination with Indian music (although he had used a sitar in John's "Norwegian Wood" the previous year). On *Sgt. Pepper's Lonely Hearts Club Band* (1967), he delivered a masterpiece, "Within You, Without You," compelling enough to become the prototype for a subgenre known as "raga rock." He also immersed himself in Indian culture, drawing the Beatles into the practice of transcendental meditation, and thus helping to set the spiritual tone of youth culture during the late 1960s. Like John's escapism and Paul's exuberance, contemplation of his place in the cosmic scheme was George's reaction to the demigodhood bestowed by the forces of Beatlemania.

Like the other Fabs, George spent short stretches of time away from the partnership during 1967 and 1968, experimenting with the newfangled Moog synthesizer on *Electronic Sounds* [US: Zapple ST-3358 (1969)] and indulging his fascination with Indian music in a film score, *Wonderwall* [US: Apple ST-3350 (1968)]. Within the group, he was writing more and better songs than ever before. For the White Album he delivered "While My Guitar Gently Weeps," "Piggies," "Savoy Truffle," and "Long, Long, Long." *Abbey Road* (1969) included two of his best, "Here Comes the Sun" and "Something," both equal in every way to the Lennon-McCartney songs on the album.

John and Paul allowed George only two or three songs per Beatle LP, and over the years he had accumulated an impressive backlog of compositions. His pent-up musical energies exploded following the group's demise, yielding the triple LP *All Things Must Pass* [CD: Parlophone CDP 7 46688/9 2 (1970)] and the star-studded benefit for East Indian refugees, *The Concert for Bangladesh* [US: Apple SCTX-3385 (1971)].

George's music became less and less prominent during the late 1970s and early 1980s. Handmade Films, a production company George founded in 1978 in order to complete Monty Python's *Life of Brian,* absorbed increasing amounts of his attention, and in 1982 he announced his retirement from the music industry.

Just when it seemed that he might never record again, George suddenly revitalized his career in 1988 with a strong new album, *Cloud Nine* [CD: Dark Horse 9 25643-2 (1988)], and a chart-topping single, "Got My Mind Set on You." Hot on its heels came *The Traveling Wilburys, Volume 1,* a superstar collaboration in which George joined forces with Tom Petty, Jeff Lynne (of Electric Light Orchestra), Roy Orbison, and Bob Dylan. That album garnered a well-deserved Grammy Award for the best rock performance of 1988. The Wilburys also contributed to the superstar charity compilation *Nobody's Child: Romanian Angel Appeal* [CD: Warner Bros. 92628 02 (1990)], on which they perform "Nobody's Child," a song that was originally recorded by the Beatles with Tony Sheridan in 1961.

With his newfound musical vitality, George, like Paul (and John immediately before his death), seemed to have finally come to terms with his status as an ex-Beatle, ready to play an active role in popular music, neither as a competitor in chart warfare, nor as a nostalgia act, but as a respected elder statesman.

Above: George on *The Magical Mystery Tour* set, September 1967. Opposite, top: George and Patti Boyd relaxing between scenes during the filming of *Help!,* 1965. Opposite, bottom: A promotional shot of George from the White Album.

We used to have good fun at press conferences. They used to be really great because there would always be somebody with a wisecrack. I do miss that side of the Fab Four, I admit.

—Press conference, Toronto, February 1988, reprinted in *Dark Horse: The Private Life of George Harrison* by Geoffrey Guiliano, 1990

I knew school wasn't the be-all and end-all of life's opportunities. That's why it didn't bother me much. There was always that side of me in school which thought, "Well, if that's what it is, then I don't want it."

—*I Me Mine* by George Harrison with Derek Taylor, 1980

There was this big skiffle craze happening for a while in England, which was Lonnie Donegan. He set all them kids on the road. Everybody was in a skiffle group. Some gave up, but the ones who didn't give up became all those bands out of the early '60s. . . . All you needed was an acoustic guitar, a washboard with thimbles for percussion, and a tea chest—you know, a box that they used to ship tea in from India—and you just put a broom handle on it and a bit of string, and you had a bass. . . . You only needed two chords: jing-jinga-jing jing-jinga-jing, jing-jinga-jing jing-jinga-jing. And I think that is basically where I've always been at. I'm just a skiffler, you know. Now I do posh skiffle. That's all it is.

—*Guitar Player* magazine, November 1987

Above and below, right: George celebrates his twenty-first birthday, February 25, 1964.

George (circa 1966).

We went to Hamburg [in 1960] and got straight into the leather gear. . . . [We were] always foaming at the mouth because they used to feed us these uppers to keep us going, because they made us work eight or ten hours a night.

—*Guitar Player* magazine, November 1987

When Lee Marvin drives up with his motorcycle gang [in the late-1950s teen movie The Wild Ones*], if my ears weren't tricking me, I could have sworn that when Lee Marvin was talking to Marlon Brando, Lee Marvin said to him, "Look, Johnny, I think such-and-such, the Beatles think that you're such-and-such"—as if his motorcycle gang was called the Beatles.*

—Unidentified radio broadcast included on *Re-Introducing The Beatles* [bootleg LP: *Rubber Soul* SAPCOR 28 (c.1988)].

We had felt cocky and certain, but when [Brian] Epstein said, "You're going to be bigger than Elvis, you know," we thought "Well, how big do you have to be? I mean, I doubt that."

—*I Me Mine* by George Harrison with Derek Taylor, 1980

[The pilot of the Beatles' chartered airplane] said that when we had finished the tour, the plane, its tail, its wings were full of bullet holes, and he said: "These crazy guys . . . they were at the end of the runway trying to pot us off." Jealous boyfriends had come down with pistols and rifles trying to kill us.

—*I Me Mine* by George Harrison with Derek Taylor, 1980

Ringo Starr

A sickly child since his birth on July 7, 1940, Richard Starkey spent much of his youth in hospitals recovering from an unfortunate series of ailments: a burst appendix that sent him into a coma, then broken bones, and later pleurisy. By the time he was fifteen he had missed so much school that he could barely read or write, and went to work tending bar on ferry boats that serviced the Mersey River. During that time, his stepfather bought him a drum kit and he joined in the skiffle craze that held British youth in its thrall.

As the Merseyside club scene began to take root, Richie, as he was known then, and as friends and family still refer to him, began playing full-time. His finesse with a back-beat landed him a spot in one of Liverpool's most popular bands, Rory Storm and the Hurricanes. To match the flashier stage names of the other members of the band, he changed his name to Ringo Starr. The Hurricanes were his ticket to fame—or to Hamburg, anyway. There, Ringo spent many a night carousing with his Liverpool mates, the Beatles, and even sat in for Pete Best when he was ill.

By 1962, however, the Hurricanes' popularity was on the wane. The clubs of Liverpool and Hamburg hadn't brought them that ticket to national exposure, a record contract, and at the age of twenty-two, Ringo felt he was becoming too old to dally with music. He had resolved to quit and learn a trade when he got a message from John, Paul, and George asking him to join the Beatles.

Joining the Fab Four on the eve of their rise to unprecedented fame, Ringo was the odd man out—a hired hand rather than a childhood friend. As Rory Storm observed, "During the four or five years Ringo was with us he really played drums—he drove them. He sweated and swung and sung. Ringo sang about five numbers a night, he even had his own spot—it was called 'Ringo Starrtime.' Now he's only a backing drummer." But if he was in the background, the drummer's presence was nonetheless essential to the Fabs. Both in public and, it appears, privately, Ringo's unassuming, good-natured personality provided a crucial balance between John's razor-sharp wit, Paul's stagey coyness, and George's sombre posturing.

As the 1960s progressed and the Beatles' musical interests propelled them further into the studio, Ringo found himself with less and less to do. While John and Paul were working on arrangements and George was adjusting his guitar sound, Ringo was in the corner playing cards with Mal Evans for hours on end. With the advent of multitrack recording technology, Paul proved capable of playing the drum parts himself, and became insistent that they be played precisely as he would play them. By the time of the White Album in 1968, with the other three Beatles producing masterpieces daily, Ringo felt distinctly expendable.

After a particularly tense session on August 22, 1968, he quit the band. The Beatles weathered the storm, recording "Back in the USSR" the next day with Paul behind the drum kit. However, the band managed to persuade Ringo to return within a few days.

In view of these developments, the drummer began to explore career alternatives. Critics had noted his performances in *Help!* and *A Hard Day's Night,* singling out his unaffected comic flair. Ringo managed to parlay this asset into a minor role in *Candy* in 1968, followed the next year by a lead opposite Peter Sellers in *The Magic Christian.* This led to appearances in *That'll Be the Day* (1973), *Sextette* (1976), *Caveman* (1981), and *Princess Daisy* (1983).

After the breakup in 1969, like his ex-bandmates, Ringo made a string of solo albums, and by 1973 seemed to have hit his stride. Inviting John, Paul, and George to contribute songs and performances, he pulled off something akin to a Beatles reunion on *Ringo* [US: Apple SWAL 3413], which yielded several hit singles: "Photograph" (Starkey-Harrison), "You're Sixteen" (Sherman-Sherman), and "Oh My My" (Starkey-Poncia). The success proved short-lived, however, and over the next seven albums Ringo's recording career foundered on changing times, mediocre material, and his own increasing self-indulgence. (His most recent release, *Old Wave* [Canada: RCA DXL 1-3233 (1983)] received no distribution in either the U.S. or the U.K.)

In October 1988, Ringo and his second wife, actress Barbara Bach, checked into a clinic in Arizona for the rehabilitation of substance abusers. One month later, the drummer and his wife emerged victorious and reenergized.

The crowning event in Ringo's personal resurgence was the announcement of a concert tour—the first of his solo career, two decades after the Beatles—with the All-Starr Band, featuring such rock'n'roll legends as Joe Walsh, Clarence Clemons, Levon Helm, Dr. John, and Billy Preston. Shows from the first leg of the tour in July 1989 were filmed and recorded, and there was talk of recording the band in a studio once a live album was released. The All-Starr Band's rendition of "With a Little Help From My Friends" can be heard on the charity compilation *Nobody's Child: Romanian Angel Appeal* [CD: Warner Bros. 92628 02 (1990)].

Above: Ringo on stage in 1964. Opposite, top: Arriving in Paris, 1964. Opposite, bottom: Ringo (circa 1968).

I'm Mr. Show Business. I'm about the most show business of the group, you know. I quite enjoy all that, entertaining.

—The Beatles Tapes: From the David Wigg Interviews, **July 1970**

I became a drummer because it was the only thing I could do. But whenever I hear another drummer, I know I'm no good.... I'm not good on the technical things, but I'm good with all the motions, swinging my head, like.

—The Beatles in Their Own Words, **various sources, compiled by Barry Miles, 1978**

Ringo on holiday in Tobago in late 1966.

From various press conferences:

Reporter: *Beethoven figures in one of your songs. What do you think of Beethoven?*
Ringo: *He's great. Especially his poetry.*
Reporter: *What did you think when your airliner's engine began smoking as you landed today?*
Ringo: *Beatles, women and children first!*
Reporter: *Why do you think you get more fan mail than anyone else in the group?*
Ringo: *I don't know. I suppose it's because more people write me.*
Reporter: *How do you like this welcome?*
Ringo: *So this is America. They all seem out of their minds.*

—*The Beatles in Their Own Words*, various sources,
compiled by Barry Miles, 1978

When we first started, we were the nice clean moptops and every mother's son and everyone loved us. And then suddenly there's a few things that they don't understand and that they don't get, and that they don't like, and so it turns them off us a bit. But I still think we're very popular. It's just that we're men now, we're a bit older than those lads that started out, and we've got a lot of things to do. You've got to do a few of them, it doesn't matter what people say. You can't live all your life by what they want. We can't go on forever as four clean little moptops playing "She Loves You."

—*The Beatles Tapes: From the David Wigg Interviews*, December 1968

There's that famous saying, "You always hurt the one you love." And we all love each other, and we all know that, but we still sort of hurt each other occasionally. You know, we just misunderstand each other.

—*The Beatles Tapes: From the David Wigg Interviews*, December 1968

[The Beatle era] was the worst time, and the best time, in my life. The best time because we played a lot of good music and had a lot of good times, and the worst time because touring is never a pleasure. Playing was always the pleasure, but what goes with it, you know, especially for a group as big as us, it was like 24 hours a day with no break—press, people fighting to get into your room, climbing 25 stories up drainpipes, knocking on your window. It never stopped.... If we'd carried on, I personally would have gone insane.

—*The Beatles Tapes: From the David Wigg Interviews*, July 1970

[During concerts], no one knew if it was good or bad.... You feel like, "What am I doing? I'm playing the biggest load of shit in the world, and people are standing and cheering."

—*The Beatles Tapes: From the David Wigg Interviews*, July 1970

On quitting the Beatles during the recording of the White Album:

I felt like I was playing like shit. And those three were really getting on. I had this feeling that nobody loved me. I felt horrible. So I said to myself, "What am I doing here? Those three are getting along so well, and I'm not even playing well...." That was madness, so I went away on holiday to sort things out. I don't know, maybe I was just paranoid. You know that to play in a band you have to trust each other.

—*The Big Beat: Conversations with Rock's Great Drummers* by Max Weinberg with Robert Santelli, 1984, quoted in *Beatlesongs* by William J. Dowlding, 1989

Above: Ringo leaves the hospital following his tonsillectomy in December 1964. Top, right: On the *Help!* set in Nassau, spring 1965.

Beatle People
Fifth Beatles

Many people have earned the title "Fifth Beatle." These people were usually loyal companions such as road manager Mal Evans, manager Brian Epstein, and producer George Martin. In addition, a number of people have appointed themselves Fifth Beatles, usually quite undeservedly, in attempts to cash in on the Fab Four's popularity. But there are also a number of musicians who were, in fact, fifth (or sixth) Beatles, and accompanied John, Paul, George, and/or Ringo at various times during their career.

These are the true Fifth Beatles:

Pete Best: Drummer for Liverpool's Black Jacks, and son of Mona Best, owner of the Casbah Club, Best often sat in with the Quarry Men when they played the Casbah. On the eve of their first trip to Hamburg in August 1960, John, Paul, and George asked Best to come along. He jumped at the opportunity.

Thus, Best became the Beatles' first official drummer. From the start, it was clear that he didn't quite fit in. Shy and taciturn, he would often sit quietly at a bar or stay at home while the other three engaged in wild exploits throughout the Reeperbahn, Hamburg's red-light district. Certainly, he was the most handsome of the four. It has been reported that he was the most popular with Liverpool's female population. Some people even say that was why his tenure as a Beatle was so abruptly terminated.

Although the full story remains unclear, shortly after their first visit to EMI's Abbey Road studio in June 1962 (during which producer George Martin had suggested that the band would need to hire a studio drummer for recording sessions), Brian Epstein called Best into his office and told him that the others wanted him out of the group. Best was crushed, and fans in Liverpool were shocked and angry.

Best's post-Beatle career with the All Stars and the Pete Best Four continued his pattern of big breaks followed by bitter disappointments, driving him into a severe depression during which he attempted suicide. Eventually, he took a job at a Liverpool bakery. In a February 1965 interview in *Playboy,* Ringo cruelly (though offhandedly) suggested that Best's drumming had been adversely affected by drug abuse. The ex-Beatle sued for libel. He has attempted periodic revivals of his musical career, making the rounds on the TV talk show circuit, often in conjunction with reissues of the Beatles' 1961 Hamburg recordings. His autobiography, *Beatle! The Pete Best Story,* was published by Plexus in 1982.

Ken Brown: John, Paul, and George weren't very busy in August 1959, so George began moon-

The early Beatles, with Pete Best at the drums.

lighting with the Les Stewart Quartet. The Quartet's rhythm guitarist, Ken Brown, had managed to secure a booking for the group at the Casbah on the club's opening night. Unfortunately, he missed a few rehearsals in the process. In the subsequent row, bandleader Les Stewart refused to play the gig. Ken then invited George, John, and Paul to join him, and as the Quarry Men, they became a regular attraction at the Casbah.

Brown, however, didn't last long. One night when he was ill, the trio performed without him. Club owner Mona Best felt he should be paid anyway, but John and Paul didn't agree. Getting rid of Brown turned out to be the simplest solution.

Eric Clapton: One of the finest guitarists to have emerged from the early 1960s "British Invasion" of the U.S., and to this day one of George's closest friends (despite the role he played in the dissolution of George's first marriage to Patricia Anne Boyd). George invited him to join the Beatles during the recording of "While My Guitar Gently Weeps" on the White Album. He felt that the presence of an outsider would ease tensions among the band by "putting them on their best behavior." (This strategy must have worked; during the making of *Let It Be,* he brought in Billy Preston.)

Incidentally, Clapton bears the unique distinction of having played on solo projects by all four ex-Beatles: John's *Live Peace in Toronto 1969* [US: Apple SW-3362], George's *Dark Horse* [US: Apple SMAS-3418 (1974)], Ringo's *Rotogravure* [US: Atlantic SD-18193 (1976)], and Wings' *Back to the Egg* [US: Columbia FC-36057 (1979)].

Johnny Gentle: When the Beatles failed an audition to back British pop singer Billy Fury in early 1960, Fury's manager Larry Parnes signed them up for a two-week tour of Scotland with singer Johnny Gentle. Their playing was not appreciated by Duncan McKinnon, the Scottish promoter who booked the tour—he intended to fire them after the first week, but was dissuaded by Gentle. Gentle himself wasn't too impressed with the Beatles (or the Silver Beatles as they called themselves on the tour), at first. "When I first saw them," he recalls, "I wondered what on earth Parnes had sent me." Gentle soon changed his mind, however, and later joined the Beatles for a few impromptu appearances in Liverpool.

Eric Clapton (circa 1968).

Johnny "Hutch" Hutchinson: One of the Mersey scene's most highly regarded drummers. Hutch played with Cass and the Cassanovas, one of the bands that took part in the Billy Fury audition. When the Beatles' drummer, Tommy Moore, failed to show up on time, Hutch took his place. Photographs of the event depict the drummer looking entirely uninterested during his moment of glory as a Fab.

Janice the Stripper: Featured performer at the New Cabaret Artists strip club in Liverpool, where the Beatles backed her during the summer of 1960. Under the refining influence of Brian Epstein, Paul would recall: "At the end of the act, she would turn around and . . . well, we were all young lads, we'd never seen anything like it before, and all blushed . . . four blushing red-faced lads." However, as *Mersey Beat* publisher Bill Harry pointed out, John and Stuart Sutcliffe, at least, had seen plenty of naked women during figure-drawing lessons at the Liverpool Art College, so Janice's act probably didn't come as such a shock.

Tommy Moore: Drummer for the Silver Beatles during their 1960 tour of Scotland with Johnny Gentle. Reportedly, he suffered a great deal of verbal abuse from John Lennon. He lost two of his front teeth when the group's van landed in a ditch; nonetheless, he was persuaded to perform that night.

After the tour he quit the band, steadfastly refusing heartfelt pleas to return to the drummerless Fabs. Moore died in 1981.

Jimmy Nichol: When Ringo collapsed with tonsillitis and pharyngitis on the eve of the Beatles' 1964 World Tour, drummer Jimmy Nichol, formerly of Georgie Fame's Blue Flames, was called in as a substitute. Over the coming weeks, whenever he was asked what it was like to be a Beatle, Nichol would reply stoically, "It's getting better." Paul and John eventually set this refrain to music on *Sgt. Pepper's Lonely Hearts Club Band*.

While on tour, Nichol took advantage of his publicly unfamiliar face, and shopped for jewelry in Hong Kong and sat in on nightclub sets in Sydney. These activities did not endear him to John, Paul, and George, who were confined to their hotel rooms. He appeared with the group in the Netherlands, Hong Kong, and Australia before being thrust back into obscurity upon Ringo's return. He didn't awaken the Fabs to say goodbye on the morning of his return to Britain.

Despite great hopes that his tenure as a Beatle would bring fame and fortune, Nichol landed in bankruptcy court on April 29, 1965, with debits of £4,066 and assets of £50.

Billy Preston: The single release of "Get Back" attributes the record to "the Beatles with Billy Preston," making the American keyboardist the only outside musician to have been credited on a Beatle record. For all practical purposes, Preston

was accepted as a full-fledged member of the band during many of the sessions for *Let It Be* and *Abbey Road*. His electric piano solos grace "Get Back" and "Don't Let Me Down," and the Beatles even recorded two of his songs, although the recordings remain unreleased. In addition to providing Apple Records with a number of its non-Beatle hits, Preston performed on several solo efforts by John, George, and Ringo.

Ronnie the Hood: On June 11, 1960, during one of their intermittent drummerless periods, the Silver Beatles played the Grosvenor Ballroom in Cheshire. Having set up a borrowed drum kit, they invited any member of the audience to play the kit. Ronnie, a local hood, took the stage. Repeated attempts to dissaude him met with failure and threats of violence. He enjoyed drumming with the Silver Beatles so much that he almost didn't leave. Finally, Allan Williams was summoned, and he effectively removed Ronnie from the stage.

Tony Sheridan: London guitarist and vocalist who became the first British rock'n'roller to play in Hamburg, initiating the chain of events that brought the Beatles international fame.

A friend of Sheridan's encountered German entrepreneur Bruno Koschmeider while the latter was looking for bands to book into his Hamburg clubs. Although he didn't have a band, he told the club owner that he was a member of "The Jets," a band that didn't even exist. Easily convinced, Koschmeider hired them, and in May 1960 the band, fronted by Sheridan, debuted at the Kaiserkeller.

Sheridan then became a regular at the Top Ten Club and used Mersey bands to back him up. During their second trip to Hamburg, the Beatles joined him for two Polydor recording sessions produced by Bert Kaempfert, which resulted in the Fabs' first commercial release, "My Bonnie (Lies Over the Ocean)." Enthusiastic reviews in Liverpool's music newspaper, *Mersey Beat,* turned the record into a minor hit, and it was this attention that led Brian Epstein to attend a performance of the Beatles at the Cavern Club.

Stuart Sutcliffe: The Quarry Men's first electric bass player, and the person who suggested the name Beetles (John later added the 'a'). A genuinely brilliant painter, he and John became best friends while the two of them were attending Liverpool Art College in 1959. As a member of the Student Union Committee (along with *Mersey Beat* founder Bill Harry), he appropriated College money to buy a public address system so that the Quarry Men could play school dances. The group later sold the system in Germany, which got them in trouble with the College.

Sutcliffe was attracted to the Beatles by John's rock'n'roll affectations, and, spurred on by John, bought a bass using money from the sale of his first painting, even though he had had no prior musical experience. Soon thereafter, he joined

Paul and Stuart Sutcliffe.

John, Paul, George, Tommy Moore, and Johnny Gentle on their 1960 tour of Scotland.

During the group's first trip to Hamburg in August 1960, Sutcliffe fell in love with German photographer Astrid Kirchherr, and elected to remain there to study art after their second trip. Over the following months, he suffered from mysterious and excruciating headaches. When the Beatles arrived for their third stint in Hamburg in April 1962, they found that their dear friend had died two days earlier of a brain hemorrhage.

Since his death, Sutcliffe's mother has worked tirelessly to establish her son's reputation as one of Liverpool's finest artists through exhibitions of his work.

Ivan Vaughn: Occasional tea-chest bass player, and later, manager of the Quarry Men. Vaughn was the mutual friend who brought Paul to see John perform at the Woolton Fete on July 6, 1957.

Lu Walters: Born Walter Eymund, Lu Walters was the bass player with Rory Storm and the Hurricanes. Walters invited the Beatles to join him and the Hurricanes for a recording session, which he set up to feature his talents as a vocalist. Pete Best was ill on the day of the session, October 15, 1960, so Hurricane Ringo Starr sat in. This was the first recording to include all four of the future Fabs, but the products of the session have never been released, nor have they surfaced in bootleg form.

Andy White: Dissatisfied with Ringo's performance on the Beatles' initial recording of "Love Me Do," producer George Martin hired Andy White, a London session drummer, to play at a subsequent recording session. Both versions of the song have been released; White's is marked by a tambourine part, played by the dejected Ringo. White can also be heard on the only available recording of "P.S. I Love You."

Beatle Family Members

Obviously, family members are a critical aspect of the Beatles' story. John's mother Julia, for example, was a noticeable force in his music, while others, such as Ringo's stepfather Harry Graves, made more subtle contributions. Here are a number of family members who played a significant role in the Beatles' lives and careers:

Olivia Trinidad Arias: Second wife of George Harrison, whom she married in September 1978. The two met in 1974 while Olivia was a secretary at A&M Records, distributor for George's Dark Horse label at the time. She is the mother of his only child, son Dhani (whose name means "wealth" in Hindi), born on August 1, 1978.

Barbara Bach: American actress who rose to prominence starring opposite Roger Moore's James Bond in *The Spy Who Loved Me*. She met costar Ringo Starr on the set of *Caveman* in 1981; shortly thereafter they married. She has appeared in Ringo's short film *The Cooler* (1982) and in Paul's movie *Give My Regards to Broad Street* (1984).

Patricia Anne Boyd: Having appeared in TV commercials under the direction of Richard Lester, Patti Boyd was hired by the director as an extra in the Beatles' first film, *A Hard Day's Night*. Her romance with George Harrison blossomed quickly, and they were wed on January 21, 1966. It was Patti's interest in transcendental meditation that brought the Maharishi Mehesh Yogi to George's attention.

Their relationship eventually soured, and George's peer and close friend Eric Clapton fell in love with Mrs. Harrison. (Clapton's song "Layla," one of the most impassioned performances in rock'n'roll, describes his feelings for her.) Patti and Eric were married in March 1979. George commented philosophically, "I'd rather she was with him than some dope."

George with Patti Boyd Harrison in 1967.

Ringo with Maureen Cox Starkey in 1965.

Maureen Cox: Ringo's second wife, a Liverpool hairdresser and Beatle fan. By her own account, the first time she met Ringo was when she asked him for his autograph. They met again when Maureen kissed him on a dare, after which he asked her to dance. They were married on February 11, 1965. She is the mother of Ringo's sons Zak (born on September 13, 1965) and Jason (born on August 19, 1967), and daughter Lee Starkey (born on November 11, 1970). Ringo's infidelities eventually caused her to sue for divorce, which was granted July 1975.

Maureen sang, along with Yoko, during the chorus of "Bungalow Bill" on the White Album; Paul can be heard thanking her ("Thanks, Mo!") for her enthusiastic applause at the end of "Get Back" on the *Let It Be* album.

Linda Eastman: Wife of Paul McCartney. Contrary to widespread belief, Linda's family is not the Eastman family of Eastman-Kodak; her family's name, changed by her father, was originally Epstein.

Linda grew up in an affluent suburb of New York City, attended rock concerts at the Brooklyn Paramount, and sang in a vocal trio. After an unsuccessful marriage, she took a job as a receptionist at *Town and Country* magazine. Around this time, she began to spice up her social life by meeting rock stars as they passed through town, and she often took their pictures. Her photographs began to attract attention and became widely published in the rock press.

After meeting Paul at a press conference, she pursued him doggedly. She slipped him her phone number, sent him personalized photocollages, and even flew to London on the pretext of a photographic assignment. Paul suddenly began taking her seriously after a period of dalliance, and eventually she moved into his London home

with her daughter from a previous marriage, Heather. The couple wed on March 12, 1969; their first child, Mary, was born on August 29, 1969. Daughter Stella was born on September 13, 1971, and son James Louis on September 12, 1977.

After the breakup of the Beatles, Paul convinced his wife to play in his band, and Linda, then twenty-nine, taught herself to play keyboards. Although she gave up her professional aspirations as a photographer when she married Paul, books of her photographs were published in 1976 and 1982. In addition, she has published a vegetarian cookbook. Her own composition, "Seaside Woman," was released in 1977 under the name Suzy and the Red Stripes [US: Epic 8-50403].

Linda continues to join her husband onstage, and played keyboards with the Paul McCartney Band on their 1989–1990 World Tour.

Louise Harrison: Mother of George and his siblings Louise, Harold, and Peter. To the disgust of John's Aunt Mimi, Mrs. Harrison supported her son's musical endeavors wholeheartedly, and attended his performances throughout the early days. As Beatlemania spread, she and George's father played the role of Beatle parents to the hilt, answering fan mail, interviewing with the press, and representing their son at civic receptions.

Maureen leaves the hospital with her newborn son Jason in 1967.

Alfred Lennon: Father of John, known as Freddie. At age six, John was asked to choose between his mother and his father. When he chose to remain with Julia, Freddie disappeared; he resurfaced only when the *Sunday Express* sought him out in an attempt to reunite him with John in 1964. The reunion took place, but it was not a success. In 1965, he recorded an autobiographical song, "That's My Life (My Home and My Love)" [UK: Jerden 792], a move widely interpreted as an attempt to cash in on John's fame. During the 1970s, the two resumed contact, and are said to have been on friendly terms at the time of Freddie's death in 1976.

Life magazine documents Paul's existence in this 1969 cover photograph. He is shown with his wife, Linda Eastman McCartney, daughter Heather, and baby Mary.

John Charles Julian Lennon: John's first son by his first wife Cynthia, born on April 8, 1963, and named for John's late mother Julia. Julian's contribution to the Beatles is not insignificant: His title for a drawing he made at age four inspired John's song "Lucy in the Sky with Diamonds," and Paul's "Hey Jude" began as "Hey Jules," a reassurance to the child during the difficult period following his parents' divorce. In addition, one of Julian's drawings adorned the cover of the Beatles 1967 Christmas record, which was distributed to Fan Club members.

For much of Julian's childhood, his famous father was absent or preoccupied with the Beatles and, later, with his second wife Yoko Ono. Nonetheless, Julian took an interest in rock'n'roll, played guitar in bands and eventually released records under his own name. His first single, "Valotte" [from *Valotte*, CD: Atlantic 80184-1] sounded uncannily like his father's music of the late 1960s and was an immediate hit. He has yet to repeat that success.

Julia Stanley Lennon: Mother of John and his half-sisters Julia, Jacqueline, and Victoria. Julia's impact on John's character is inestimable: She contributed to both the irreverent, carefree spirit that led him into a life of music and iconoclasm, as well as to the insecurity that left him emotionally scarred throughout most of his life.

Having placed him in the care of her sister Mimi during infancy, Julia reestablished a relationship with John when he was a teenager; she played host to his friends and taught him his first

songs on the banjo. He showed little emotion when she was killed in a car accident outside of Mimi's home on July 15, 1958. Years later, however, he acknowledged that losing his mother was one of the most significant events of his life. Julia's presence haunts such songs as "Julia" and "Mother."

Sean Taro Lennon: John's second son, the only child of John Lennon and Yoko Ono, born on October 9, 1975. John abandoned his musical career in favor of spending time at home with Sean during the child's first five years. Sean speaks about his father in the documentary film *Imagine: John Lennon* (1988).

James McCartney: Father of Paul and Michael McCartney. A sometime bandleader, he formed both the Masked Melody Makers and the Jim Mac Band. Paul recorded his father's instrumental composition "Walking in the Park with Eloise" [US: EMI 3977] in 1974 under the name the Country Hams.

Paul with his father, Jim McCartney, late 1967.

John and Julian explore Scotland with Yoko and Kyoko, July 1969.

Mary Patricia Mohin McCartney: Mother of Paul and Michael McCartney. Like John's mother Julia, Mary died while Paul was a teenager, of breast cancer. Paul recalls her "speaking words of wisdom" in the song "Let It Be."

Michael McCartney, a.k.a. **Mike McGear:** Trying to stay out of his brother's shadow, Michael McCartney has pursued an active musical career under the name Mike McGear. He has recorded with various music-and-humor ensembles including Scaffold, McGear and McGough, Grimms, and under his own name. In addition, he has published children's books as well as a book of family reminiscences and photographs, *The Macs* (Delilah/Putnam's, 1981).

Yoko Ono: John's second wife, often unfairly blamed for the breakup of the Beatles, and by far the most ambiguous character in the entire Beatle drama. In a 1974 magazine article published in Japan, she described herself in these terms:

> I am a fish on a cutting board. I feel tormented because I'm out of water. I'm breathing hard because I'm out of oxygen. I want to be killed because living is painful. I want to be cut up with a knife. That's the vision I have of myself.

Born in 1933 to aristocratic Japanese parents, Yoko was named "Ocean Child" because her

Look magazine features John and Yoko.

50 CENTS · MARCH 18, 1969

LOOK

LENNON & ONO, INC.
Beatle John and his girl friend join forces—and POW!

MICKEY MANTLE
His toughest decision

IRISH ISLES
a St. Patrick's

father transferred across the Pacific, to the San Francisco office of Yokohama Specie Bank, two weeks before her birth. Although she spent a few childhood years in the U.S., she returned to Japan in 1941 just before fighting broke out and, like John, grew up amidst the bombs and sirens of World War II.

At the age of eighteen, Yoko moved to Scarsdale, New York, and enrolled as a student of philosophy at Sarah Lawrence College. After graduation, she introduced her artistic concepts to the Greenwich Village art scene, joining the Fluxus group of artists that nurtured such luminaries as Nam June Paik, LaMonte Young, and George Maciunas. Many of her works were performance pieces often involving audience participation; in a piece presented in 1965 at New York's Carnegie Hall (Carnegie Recital Hall, that is, an adjunct to the famous venue), spectators snipped off swatches of her clothing as she sat quietly onstage.

Yoko's six-year marriage to composer Toshi Ichianagi was followed by seven years as the wife of Tony Cox, with whom she made a number of avant-garde films and had one child, daughter Kyoko. By the time she met John Lennon in November 1966, Yoko had already pursued an active career as a multimedia artist in New York, London, and Tokyo. In one-time appearances with such luminaries as jazz saxophonist Ornette Coleman, she had also begun to develop the use of her voice as an engine for producing abstract sounds, more like the gasping cries of an infant than conventional singing.

With the creation of John and Yoko's *Unfinished Music No. 1: Two Virgins* [US: Apple T-5001 (1968)], it was only natural that Yoko become an Apple recording artist. She adopted the practice of planning her albums in tandem with John's, so that with each Lennon release, an accompanying Ono release would provide counterpoint from an avant-garde perspective. As she and John were drawn more deeply into populist politics, and as public recognition of her talents failed to materialize, Yoko's music became less abstract. In recent times her records have come to consist of conventional, if not very attractive, pop songs.

It's impossible not to recognize, and difficult not to respect, the profound effect Yoko had on John. He chose her as one of only two long-term collaborators in his life, not to mention the many impassioned defenses of her character and talents which he felt called upon to make. As long as they were together (and even, it seems, while they were apart during 1974), John regarded his relationship with Yoko as the center of his personal universe. Since his death, she has maintained a low profile, donating large sums of money to charitable causes, contributing pieces to art exhibitions, and recording occasionally.

Cynthia Powell: John's first wife, whom he met while he was a student at the Liverpool Art College. Her staid demeanor contrasted sharply with John's rebelliousness, but the romance was

Top: John and Cynthia Powell Lennon (circa 1964). Bottom: John and Cynthia at Foyle's Literary Luncheon, April 1964, where John received honors for his book *In His Own Write.*

stable. They were married in August 1962, well before the Beatles' ascendence to international fame.

Cynthia endured two difficult years as the secret wife of John Lennon and mother of his child while her husband was caught up in the whirlwind of Beatlemania. After coming out of hiding, she spent several more difficult years in public as the wife of one of the most celebrated entertainers in the history of the world.

Returning from a solitary vacation in Greece in 1968, she found Yoko Ono wearing one of her

bathrobes. Cynthia has since remarried and divorced twice. Her autobiography, *A Twist of Lennon,* was published by Star Books/W.H. Allen in 1978, and she recently opened a restaurant, Lennon's, in London.

Mimi Stanley Smith: John simultaneously revered and dreaded his Aunt Mimi, in whose care he was placed as an infant. She strove to provide a comfortable and loving environment for him, but inevitably this strict upbringing clashed with John's rebelliousness. A stern but reasonable woman, she is best remembered by fans for her statement, "A guitar's all right, John, but you'll never earn a living by it."

Elsie Gleave Starkey: Ringo's mother, who raised him single-handedly after his father left in 1943, when Ringo was three. She remarried in 1953. Her second husband, Harry Graves, bought Ringo his first drum kit.

Zak Starkey: Ringo's eldest son, born on September 13, 1965. His artwork graces the cover of the Beatles' 1969 Christmas record. He has appeared playing drums during some of his father's 1989 concerts.

Friends and Lovers

A number of personal friends have made important contributions to the Beatles' careers. Some, like the Maharishi, brought ideas into the group that later proved influential. Star-Club bouncer Horst Fascher was simply there to lend a hand at crucial moments. (Many friends went on to become important business associates, and are listed under that heading.)

Jane Asher: Successful British actress and sister of Apple executive Peter Asher. Asher was Paul's steady girlfriend, and later his fiancée, between 1963 and 1968. His most poignant love songs from those years were inspired by her, including "Here, There, and Everywhere," which Paul still cites as one of his favorites.

Only a short time after announcing their plans to marry, their relationship dissolved suddenly—probably as a result of Paul's periodic infidelities. Afterwards, Asher continued to pursue her acting career, and has appeared in the title role of the London stage production of *Peter Pan,* in the film *Alfie,* and in the television production of *Brideshead Revisited.*

Horst Fascher: Bouncer at the Kaiserkeller, and later at the Top Ten Club and Star-Club, both locales at which the Beatles played during their trips to Hamburg. A former boxer once imprisoned for manslaughter, Fascher looked after the Beatles while they were in Hamburg, and steered them clear of trouble with the numerous pimps, drug peddlers, and gangsters who operated in the Reeperbahn.

Astrid Kirchherr: German photographer and girlfriend of Klaus Voorman, and later of Stuart Sutcliffe. Kirchherr is generally credited with having originated the Beatle haircut—an oversimplification, as many Liverpool art students wore their hair long—and with pioneering the play of light and shadow that formed the basis of the cover photo for *With the Beatles.*

Maharishi Mehesh Yogi: Born Mehesh Prasad Varma, the Maharishi was one of the many momentary but profound influences on John Lennon, and a lifelong spiritual influence upon George Harrison. Despite George Harrison's protestations that the Maharishi was "not a modern man," the Maharishi had obtained a degree in physics in 1942 and proved to be quite effective at transforming the Beatles' interest in transcendental meditation into publicity for his Spiritual Regeneration movement.

After an introductory course in transcendental meditation in Wales, all four Beatles traveled to the Maharishi's retreat in Rishikesh, India. Ringo returned within a matter of days, reporting that the food was too spicy for his sensitive stomach (a legitimate complaint for a man who had spent his childhood beset by gastrointestinal ailments). Paul returned a short time later; during the *Get Back/Let It Be* sessions, he recalled that the experience was like his days at the Quarry Bank High School. George also left the Maharishi's camp prematurely, but the Indian metaphysics he studied there made a lasting impression.

Unfortunately, the episode ended bitterly when, hearing stories of the yogi's sexual advances toward one of the female disciples, John decided that the Maharishi had betrayed his trust. Confronted by an angry Lennon, the Maharishi asked what was wrong. John replied, "If you're so cosmic, you'll know." On the White Album, John vented his anger toward the Maharishi, but disguised the holy man's name as "Sexy Sadie": "Sexy Sadie, what have you done?/You made a fool of everyone."

Alexis Mardas, a.k.a. **Magic Alex:** A close friend of John's during the late 1960s, and one of the most notorious of the sycophants who bilked Apple Corps. It was Magic Alex whose unsubstantiated reports of the Maharishi's fleshly desires led the Beatles to abandon the Maharishi in Rishikesh. He also told John of his one-night affair with Cynthia, giving John the pretext of adultery as grounds for the divorce he had been planning

Paul with Jane Asher, December 1967.

since his first night with Yoko. Then Magic Alex accepted John's assignment to deliver news of the impending divorce to the soon-to-be ex-Mrs. Lennon! (The tables turned as it became clear that Yoko was pregnant, and John allowed Cynthia to bring him to court.)

Mardas was a man of many ideas, pitifully few of which came to fruition. John was impressed, initially, with his "nothing box," a small plastic cube covered with red lights which blinked on and off randomly. Promising such innovations as glowing paint that would replace overhead lighting, an artificial replacement for the sun, and a force field that would invisibly block sound waves, Mardas was appointed head of Apple Electronics and given a hefty budget.

The farce came to an abrupt halt in mid-January 1969 when the Beatles left Twickenham Studios, where they had been rehearsing material for what became the *Let It Be* album, to record in their own new 72-track Apple Recording Studio, designed and constructed by Mardas. They arrived to find the studio filled with crude, hand-built gadgetry, none of which worked. The materials were eventually sold as scrap.

Producer George Martin hurriedly installed mobile recording equipment rented from EMI, and Mardas, his magic finally spent, was dismissed.

Klaus Voorman: After a tiff with his girlfriend Astrid Kirchherr, art student Klaus Voorman went carousing through Hamburg's Reeperbahn. As he passed the door to the Kaiserkeller he chanced to look inside, and was transfixed by the sound and visual impact of the Beatles.

Voorman, Kirchherr, and their friends soon became the Beatles' closest friends in Germany, and Voorman remained a close friend long after the Beatles became a household name. His artwork for the *Revolver* cover won a Grammy Award; he also illustrated the cover for George's *Wonderwall Music.* In addition, Voorman's bass playing landed him gigs with the first few editions of John's early-1970s vehicle, the Plastic Ono Band.

Paul, George, and John with Maharishi Mehesh Yogi, August 1967.

Business Associates

Neil Aspinall: One of the original "Liverpool Mafia" that surrounded the Beatles throughout their career. Aspinall first met Paul and George when they were all students at the Liverpool Institute. Aspinall went on to study accounting, and while living at the home of Pete Best, bought a second-hand van and became the Beatles' road manager. Staying on after Pete Best was fired, he became the Beatles' personal assistant when Mal Evans signed on as their road manager. In January 1968 Aspinall was named managing director of Apple, and later headed Apple Films and produced the *Let It Be* movie. He continues to oversee Apple's affairs to this day.

Tony Barrow: Record reviewer for the *Liverpool Echo,* whom manager Brian Epstein asked in late 1961 for a mention of the Beatles in print. Barrow declined, explaining that he couldn't cover the band if they didn't have a record out. He did, however, refer Epstein to one of his associates at Decca Records. Epstein secured an audition with Decca on January 1, 1962. Unfortunately, the Beatles didn't pass. Despite the setback, Epstein offered Barrow a position as director of public relations for the Beatles' management, NEMS Enterprises, which he accepted. In later years, Barrow became a successful independent music-business PR man, writer of album liner notes, and ghostwriter of Beatles-related books.

Peter Brown: In 1962, Brown managed the record department of a store that competed with NEMS (Northern England Music Stores), the Epstein family's business, from which Brian later drew the name of his record company. At Epstein's invitation, the two joined forces, and soon Brown became Epstein's personal assistant. During the late 1960s he served as an executive for Apple, where he went to extraordinary lengths to arrange John's short-notice wedding to Yoko Ono. (John's "The Ballad of John and Yoko" acknowledges his efforts.) His memoir of the Beatle years, *The Love You Make,* was published in 1983.

Nicky Byrne: When a flood of unauthorized Beatle merchandise was unleashed upon the market in 1964, Brian Epstein put Nicky Byrne in charge of licensing the Beatles' names and likenesses to manufacturers. Byrne, a London club owner and notorious socialite, drew up a contract that gave his company 90 percent of the take, expecting it would serve as his initial bargaining position. Much to his surprise, NEMS Enterprises' representative signed it without question. It took Epstein six months to notice the mistake, during which time millions of dollars flowed into Byrne's pockets. In the ensuing lawsuits (which brought the manufacture and sale of Beatles merchandise to a standstill) over $100 million is estimated to have been lost.

Syd Coleman: Manager of Ardmore and Beechwood, the music publishing subsidiary of British entertainment conglomerate Electrical and Musical Industries (EMI). In the spring of 1962, Coleman received a call from Ted Huntley, who had been impressed with the Beatles music when he manufactured a few acetate disks of their Decca audition for Brian Epstein. Coleman listened to the recordings and immediately offered to publish two of the three original compositions: "Love of the Loved" and "Hello Little Girl." He passed, presumably, on "Like Dreamers Do." Next, he phoned producer George Martin, who had asked him to be on the lookout for new talent. As a result, Ardmore and Beechwood published "Love Me Do." All later Beatle songs were published in association with Dick James.

Lee Eastman: Harvard-educated attorney and father of Linda Eastman McCartney. By the time Paul met Linda in 1968, it had become clear to the Beatles that they needed a replacement for their deceased manager, Brian Epstein. Impressed with Lee Eastman's knowledge of financial affairs, Paul became convinced that he was the best man for the job.

The other Beatles didn't agree. Not only did they resent Paul's attempts to bring his father-in-law into their affairs, they had already found someone they regarded as a suitable candidate, New York dealmaker Allen Klein. Reluctantly, Paul signed the agreement placing Klein in charge of the Beatles, but retained Eastman as his personal representative. Eastman and Klein, one an upper-crust old boy, the other a self-made scrapper, often worked at cross-purposes. Their conflicts cemented the growing differences between Paul on the one hand and John, George, and Ringo on the other, and hastened the deterioration of their musical and interpersonal relationships.

Brian Epstein: The Beatles' manager between 1962 and 1967. Arguably, Epstein's faith, commitment, and imaginative management were as crucial to the Beatles' success as their music and collective personality.

Epstein bore the difficulties of being Jewish in Protestant England, and homosexual at a time when such behavior was punishable by law. By young adulthood, he had failed to find a niche; he had proven a failure at his family's furniture and appliance shop, been discharged from the Army on psychiatric grounds, and spent a brief but unhappy time in acting school. In 1959, he returned to the family business, NEMS (Northern England Music Stores).

Given a new branch store to manage, he finally seemed to have found his element. He reorganized the store and opened a record department, and took great care to keep it comprehensively stocked. A genteel man, he was drawn to classical music, and knew nothing of rock'n'roll. When a Liverpool youngster asked for a German recording by a local group called the Beatles, Epstein's interest was piqued. He arranged to drop by the nearby Cavern Club to see the group perform. From that moment, he was obsessed with the idea of becoming their manager.

Epstein convinced the group that he could make them "bigger than Elvis." He exchanged their leathers for Pierre Cardin suits, their randy humor for cuddly innocence, and their onstage mayhem for polite bows. The Beatles' following grew.

Epstein formed NEMS Enterprises in June 1962 to administer the Beatles' affairs, and soon acquired a stable of pop groups, including Gerry and the Pacemakers and Cilla Black. Success, however, did not bring Epstein happiness. As he tried to build upon his initial success, he found his empire crumbling even as it grew. The acts he plucked from Liverpool's beat clubs couldn't match the Beatles in talent or market potential, and he grew bored with being the world's most successful, but nonetheless one-time, starmaker. Pills and sexual thrill-seeking threatened to replace the Beatles as the focal points of his life.

By the mid-1960s Epstein's personal habits had become untenable. He fought bouts of depression through a roller coaster of professional triumphs and crises and handled them publicly with extreme aplomb, but grew increasingly less competent. Epstein was in the process of turning over most of his business affairs to Robert Stigwood when he succumbed to an overdose of barbiturates in the summer of 1967. His death was ruled accidental; there have been suggestions of suicide, but those closest to him confirm that the ruling is probably correct.

Brian Epstein, 1963.

Mal Evans: Often referred to as the "gentle giant," Evans was working as a bouncer at the Cavern Club when Brian Epstein offered him a job hauling equipment for the Beatles in 1963. He can be seen doing the same job, to Paul's piano accompaniment, during the opening of the film *Let It Be* (1970). Later in the film, he pounds an anvil to the beat of "Maxwell's Silver Hammer." He also appears briefly in *Help!* (1965), *Magical Mystery Tour* (1967), and the 1967 promotional film for "Hello Goodbye."

When the band stopped touring, Evans became a personal assistant and later an Apple executive. He is said to have contributed lyrics to "Fixing a Hole" and to have invented the album title *Sgt. Pepper's Lonely Hearts Club Band*. He discovered Apple recording artists Badfinger, and produced their hit single, "No Matter What."

After the breakup, Evans had difficulty establishing a new career. He drifted to Los Angeles. There, in 1976, his life came to a tragic end when, drunk and drugged on barbiturates, he waved a pistol at two policemen and was shot to death. In his book *The Love You Make*, Peter Brown relates that after Evans was cremated, his ashes were lost in the mail. "When John Lennon heard the story," he adds, "he couldn't help but quip that Mal had wound up in the dead letter department."

Sir Lew Grade: British television impresario, founder of the entertainment conglomerate ATV (Associated Television). Toward the end of the 1960s, music publisher Dick James foresaw the band coming to an end, and decided to bail out. Secretly, he sold his 23 percent share in Northern Songs (holder of the copyrights for Lennon-McCartney songs) to ATV, which already owned 12 percent. Thus ATV owned 35 percent of Northern Songs, while John, Paul, George, and Ringo held 31 percent. ATV, it was clear, intended a takeover; the race was on to acquire a controlling interest in the company.

The owners of the remaining Northern Songs stock formed a consortium and launched a bidding war between the Beatles and ATV. Allen Klein's flat-footed handling of the Beatles' business affairs, however, ultimately pushed the consortium in ATV's direction, and the Beatles lost control of their publishing company.

Grade hoped that the Beatles would keep their 31 percent stake. With an interest in the company, he reasoned, they would be more likely to continue writing music for Northern Songs, which would generate greater profits for ATV in the long run. Instead, the Beatles sold their shares in return for cash, an increasingly valuable resource, as Apple was collapsing around them.

In 1975, John accepted an offer to appear on a television special entitled *A Salute to Sir Lew Grade*. During his performance, the entire band wore masks that fit over the backs of their heads, giving each of them, effectively, two faces. It has been suggested that this was a subtle dig at the man who now owned the publishing income generated by Lennon's songs.

Mal Evans .

Ted Huntley: In April 1962, Brian Epstein brought the Beatles' Decca audition tapes to EMI's HMV division to be transferred onto acetate disks, a more convenient medium for presenting the music to record companies. It was Ted Huntley, formerly an engineer at EMI Studios, who cut the acetates. Impressed by the Beatles' music, and discovering that the songs were unpublished, he referred Epstein to Syd Coleman, manager of EMI's music publishing wing. Coleman called George Martin, who had put the word out that he was looking for talent. In July 1962, Martin finally handed the Beatles the contract they had sought for so long.

Dick James: The Beatles' music publisher. Born Richard Leon Isaac Vapnick, James entered the music business as a singer. In 1942 he recorded with the Primo Scala's Accordian Band, and in 1955 scored a hit with "Robin Hood," the theme for the British TV series of the same name. The recording, released on the Parlophone label, was produced by the young George Martin.

When Brian Epstein, unhappy with EMI publishing subsidiary Ardmore and Beechwood's less-than-energetic plugging of "Love Me Do," asked Martin to recommend a publisher, he mentioned Dick James. Epstein played James the Beatles' follow-up, "Please Please Me." Immediately, the publisher called up an old friend, producer of one of the most influential music shows on British television, *Thank Your Lucky Stars*. Upon hearing "Please Please Me" over the phone, the producer agreed to put the Beatles on the show.

After such a display of power, Epstein couldn't refuse James' offer to publish the group's compo-

sitions. James formed Northern Songs, which gave 20 percent ownership each to John and Paul, 10 percent to NEMS Enterprises, and reserved 50 percent for himself. Within a short time, this arrangement made him a millionaire.

Allen Klein: American music-business deal-maker, former manager of the Rolling Stones, Sam Cooke, and Bobby Vinton. He represented the Beatles between May 8, 1969, and March 10, 1971, when their assets were put in receivership by the British High Court.

Klein was raised in an orphanage because his family didn't have the means to take care of him. After a stint in the army, he began working as an accountant, found fertile ground in the music industry, and set about making his fortune through music publishing and artist management. While Brian Epstein was alive, Klein had stated his ambition to manage the Beatles; when, after Epstein's death, John Lennon publicly declared that he and Apple were going broke, this wily businessman stepped in to save the day.

Klein impressed John with his aggressiveness, street smarts, and thorough knowledge of the Beatles' music, and John convinced George and Ringo that he was the best candidate. Paul eventually gave in to the other Beatles. His dissatisfaction festered, though, and he began to look for a way to sever his ties to Klein.

Paul's father-in-law, Lee Eastman, convinced him that the only way out of the situation was to sue John, George, and Ringo for dissolution of the Beatles' partnership. Although the issue was a legal technicality, the suit unleashed a flood of bitterness that left deep wounds. Meanwhile, chaos reigned as competing interests scrambled to make the most of the Beatles' misfortunes. One by one their assets slipped through the Fab Four's fingers: Northern Songs, several Apple subsidiaries, NEMS Enterprises (part of which they had inherited after Brian Epstein's death), and finally, their working relationship.

To his credit, Klein renegotiated the group's contract with their original record company, EMI, and for the first time won them royalty rates commensurate with their stature in the industry. Eventually, however, his relationships with George, Ringo, and even John disintegrated into an endless merry-go-round of litigation that prompted George's comments on the subject in "Sue Me Sue You Blues" from *Living in the Material World* [US: Apple SMAS-3410 (1973)] and "This Song" from *33⅓* [US: Dark Horse DH-3005 (1976)].

These and other suits related to the demise of the Beatles, until recently, have held much of the money made during the post-Beatle years in escrow. In 1990, the last major suit was settled, bringing about the end of an era in pop music history. A detailed account of the business dealings leading up to the breakup can be found in *Apple to the Core* by Peter McCabe and Robert Schonfeld (Martin Brian & O'Keefe, 1972). Allen Klein explained his own point of view in a *Playboy* interview published in 1971.

Bruno Koschmeider: Owner of the Kaiserkeller, in 1960 the only rock'n'roll club in Hamburg, which featured London's own Tony Sheridan. That year, Koschmeider opened the Indra Club, where, through Liverpool promoter Allan Williams, he booked the Beatles. When the Beatles appeared at a rival club, the Top Ten, Koschmeider quietly informed the authorities that the English musicians were working without the proper permits. They were promptly deported. Among the items left behind in their hasty departure was Pete Best's drum kit.

Dick Rowe: Head of artists and repertoire at Decca Records. Rowe is known as "the man who turned down the Beatles." Rowe, however, insists that it was his assistant Mike Smith's decision to turn the band down, not his. George Martin put a new slant on the story by pointing out quite sensibly that not only Dick Rowe, but "everyone in England," had turned down the Beatles except himself.

Robert Stigwood: Australian manager of Cream, the Moody Blues, Jimi Hendrix, and the Bee Gees, who later produced the Broadway hits *Jesus Christ Superstar* and *Evita,* as well as the hugely successful movies *Grease* and *Saturday Night Fever.* His record label, RSO (for Robert Stigwood Organization), fostered a number of best-sellers during the disco era of the mid-1970s.

Impressed by his sharp eye for talent and his flamboyant style, Brian Epstein offered Stigwood a controlling interest in NEMS Enterprises in 1967, hoping to free himself to concentrate on the Beatles and Cilla Black. Epstein died, however, before the deal could be completed. By that time, Stigwood's egotistical independence and terse manner had made him many enemies at NEMS—including the Beatles—and he took £25,000 to leave quietly.

Ed Sullivan: The Beatles were little more than a show business rumor in America when Ed Sullivan happened to pass through London Airport on October 31, 1963, the same day the Beatles returned from their tour of Sweden. A throng of excited fans mobbed the airport, and the American variety show host was treated to a true demonstration of Beatlemania. Thus Sullivan, who had so effectively packaged Elvis Presley for the television audience, was intrigued when Brian Epstein asked him to put the group on his show. Epstein accepted only $10,000 for the two live performances and a taping for later broadcast, but insisted on top billing.

Fortunately for all concerned, during the interim between the deal and the air date, copies of "I Want to Hold Your Hand," still unreleased in the U.S., leaked across the Atlantic and were picked up by enthusiastic stateside DJs. Capitol, which had refused the first few Beatles releases, took notice. Rush-releasing the single, the record company organized a publicity blitz that brought five thousand fans to Kennedy Airport for the Fabs'

arrival and sixty thousand requests for CBS Studio 50's seven hundred seats.

Soon afterward, on February 9, 1964, the Beatles performed before 73 million viewers, the largest recorded TV audience to date, and inspired the same manic fervor they had in Britain. Beatlemania had arrived in the U.S.

With Ed Sullivan (1964).

Alistair Taylor: In 1961, Alistair Taylor was an underling at the Epstein family's NEMS store. On the night Epstein made his epochal visit to the Cavern Club, he thought that he would look more impressive if he were accompanied by a personal assistant, and Taylor was recruited for the job. Soon thereafter, Taylor acted as witness in the signing of Epstein's contract with the Beatles, and eventually became general manager of the NEMS store.

With Epstein's death and the formation of Apple Corps, Taylor was appointed Apple's "office manager and chief fixer." In 1969 he became one of many long-standing Beatle associates to be dismissed as a result of Allen Klein's effort to reorganize the corporation along more profitable lines.

Derek Taylor: The Beatles' press officer during 1964, and between 1968 and 1970. Taylor began his association with the Fab Four as a reporter for

the Liverpool's *Daily Express.* Having given the Beatles one of their first favorable concert reviews, he was awarded the task of ghostwriting a weekly column for George Harrison; eventually he ghostwrote Brian Epstein's autobiography, *A Cellarful of Noise.* Taylor's books are among the most entertaining and incisive commentaries on the life and times of the Beatles.

Taylor left the Beatles during the mid-1960s, and moved to Los Angeles to handle publicity for such clients as the Byrds, the Beach Boys, the Mamas and the Papas, and Captain Beefheart. With the formation of Apple, he returned to London, where he presided over Apple's publicity office until he lost his job due to Allen Klein's efforts to restructure the company.

Allan Williams: Liverpool impresario responsible for bringing Gene "Be-Bop-A-Lula" Vincent to Liverpool, and for booking the Beatles into Bruno Koschmeider's Indra Club in Hamburg. As Casey Jones of Cass and the Cassanovas tells the story, he had heard that Koschmeider was looking for bands to book in Hamburg. An employee at Allan Williams' Jacaranda Club, Casey had been using the phone on the sly to call Germany, hoping to land a gig.

One day, when Koschmeider called the Jacaranda looking for Casey, Williams happened to answer the phone. He told Koschmeider that he could supply as many bands as he needed.

After Derry and the Seniors proved a success in Hamburg, Williams sent the Beatles. When the Beatles booked themselves for a second stint in Hamburg at the Top Ten Club, however, they refused to pay Williams a commission—a discourtesy for which he has never forgiven them. Williams' book, *The Man Who Gave the Beatles Away,* was published in 1975.

Bob Wooler: Liverpool DJ and MC at the Cavern Club. Wooler, who had announced the Beatles dozens of times and claims to have persuaded them to add "Hippy Hippy Shake" (Romero) to their repertoire, wrote the first-ever review of the group for *Mersey Beat* in 1961. At Paul's twenty-first birthday party in 1963, Wooler insinuated that John and Brian Epstein were carrying on a homosexual affair, for which John beat him severely, sending him to the hospital with broken ribs. Brian Epstein offered him £200 not to press charges.

Derek Taylor and George at the Apple offices, 1969.

Beatle Producers

At first glance, it might appear that only one person, George Martin, ever produced a Beatle recording session, the sole exception being Phil Spector on *Let It Be*. A closer look, however, reveals that there have been other producers. As both Martin and Spector demonstrated so dramatically, a producer can have a huge impact on a group's recorded sound, not to mention their musical direction. With that in mind, here's a survey of the most influential Beatle producers. (Missing from the roster are several producers for BBC radio, including Peter Pilbeam, Jimmy Grant, Bernie Andrews, and Terry Henebery, whose role in the Fab Four's BBC recordings remains obscure.)

Kenny Everett: Born Maurice Cole, a British radio and television personality. As a DJ on pirate radio and later the BBC, Everett conducted a number of interviews with the Beatles. One particularly entertaining encounter was pressed into vinyl under the title *Una Sensazionale Intervista*. He is credited for the production of the Beatles' 1968 and 1969 Christmas records, a task which involved integrating separate messages recorded by each Beatle with pre-existing music, sound effects, and tape manipulations into a coherent, albeit madcap, whole. Everett went on to host his own television shows, and eventually returned to the BBC.

Glyn Johns: Britain's first freelance recording engineer, whose name appears on records by many of the most highly regarded bands in rock'n'roll. Though never credited on an official release, Johns served as producer on the ill-fated *Get Back* album.

Johns was invited to the Beatles' rehearsals in early January 1969 because he was one of the few rock'n'roll recording engineers in Britain who was also a member of the filmmakers' union. His job was to oversee the soundtrack of the film that was to document the making of the Beatles' next album (both of which eventually were titled *Let It Be*). When recording sessions for the album began at the Apple Recording Studio later in the month, he took his place behind the console. When the Beatles proved undisciplined and unmanageable, it appears original producer George Martin virtually abandoned the sinking ship. Left to his own devices, Johns tried to adhere to the stated concept behind the album, which was to record the Beatles live in the studio without any overdubs.

On May 28, 1969, the *Get Back* album was finished. Apple decided to delay its release, however, so that it would coincide with the opening of the film. Meanwhile, rough cuts of the film turned out to include music that wasn't on the album, so Johns was asked to select a new lineup of songs.

The Beatles on stage with George Martin, receiving one of their earliest awards.

The second version of *Get Back* was completed on January 5, 1970, but by that time the Beatles had lost all enthusiasm for the project. Nearly three months later, John and George invited Phil Spector to try his hand at assembling a new album, and Glyn Johns' work was abandoned.

Bert Kaempfert: German bandleader, best known as composer of "Strangers in the Night." As an artists and repertory man for Polydor during the early 1960s, Kaempfert came across singer Tony Sheridan at the Top Ten Club. Impressed by the Londoner's Presleyesque mannerisms, he arranged a recording session for him in June 1961. Sheridan asked the Beatles to back him in the recording, and the band was signed to a three-year contract with Polydor.

On the day of the recording session, John, Paul, George, and Pete Best didn't show up. After searching the bars of the Reeperbahn, Kaempfert found them asleep in their squalid room behind Bruno Koschmeider's Bambi Kino cinema. The producer woke them immediately, and that day they recorded Sheridan's hits "My Bonnie (Lies Over the Ocean)" (Pratt) and "The Saints" (trad., arr. Hines-Ward), as well as "Ain't She Sweet"

(Ager-Yellen, featuring John's lead vocal) and the Lennon-Harrison instrumental, "Cry for a Shadow."

When Brian Epstein, newly hired by the Beatles, queried Kaempfert regarding the status of their contract with Polydor, he replied that he was interested only in Sheridan, and released them without further obligation.

Bert Kaempfert died in January 1980.

George Martin: The Beatles' producer on all of their Parlophone/Capitol recordings, with the sole exception of *Let It Be*. Martin's contribution, minimal at first, grew over the years until his talent became a major factor in the band's musical approach.

As a child, Martin showed a keen interest in music. With little formal training, he taught himself how to play the piano, as well as sight-reading, harmony, and the classical repertoire. An interest in airplanes led him to join the British Fleet Air Arm at age seventeen, but he continued to write his own music and send his compositions to the Committee for the Promotion of New Music for evaluation. The Committee recommended him to Guildhall School of Music, where he took up oboe and studied composition.

Upon leaving Guildhall, Martin landed a job at EMI as a producer of classical recordings. Soon he was put in charge of EMI's Parlophone division, which specialized in comedy and novelties by such artists as Peter Sellers, the Goons, and the cast of *Beyond the Fringe.* A turning point occurred in Martin's career when he turned down pop vocalist Tommy Steele, whom Decca signed the day after Martin's rejection and made into a major star. Martin was looking for a hit pop act with which to redeem himself when Brian Epstein called.

Despite his classical roots, Martin was open-minded enough to recognize the creative potential of popular music. He also recognized that music wasn't necessarily the issue; of his first impression of the Beatles, he has said that he was "quite certain that their songwriting ability had no saleable future." But he was charmed by their personalities, and offered them a contract.

Impressed by the intensely focused aims of the Lennon-McCartney songwriting team, Martin stood by as their ideas developed, and helped them along wherever possible. Many of his earliest creative contributions are difficult to assess, but it is known that he sped up "Please Please Me" from a Roy Orbison drawl into a revved-up pop classic, arranged intros and endings, and played a large role in selecting which songs would appear on a given album. Later, he conceived and performed the contrapuntal piano solo during "In My Life." When the Beatles began to require nonstandard instrumentation around the time of *Revolver,* Martin scored the orchestrations. Meanwhile, he was recording orchestrated Beatle songs under his own name, making such records as *Off the Beatle Track* [UK: Parlophone PCS 3057 (1964)]. He also composed the scores for the films *A Hard Day's Night, Help!,* and *Yellow Submarine.*

Martin's involvement reached a peak in 1967 with *Sgt. Pepper's Lonely Hearts Club Band* and *Magical Mystery Tour.* By this time his job was no longer to capture the group's performances, but rather to translate the fanciful abstractions of their imaginations into recorded sound. His expertise resulted in the colliding circus organs of "Being for the Benefit of Mr. Kite!" and the surreal, schizophrenic flavor of that year's masterpiece, "Strawberry Fields Forever."

After two studio-intensive albums, the Beatles decided to concentrate once again on ensemble performances, and Martin's role receded accordingly. By 1969, the band was content to record without his supervision; the raw materials that would become *Let It Be* appear to have been created largely without his participation. When he was asked to return for *Abbey Road,* he made the group promise to surrender control over the sessions to him, and they agreed. *Abbey Road* became the best-selling record the Fab Four had made to date. Unfortunately, it was the last album they made together.

Martin's post-Beatles career has been marked by acclaimed productions such as *Icarus* by the Paul Winter Consort [US: Epic KE 31643 (1972)] and *Blow by Blow* by Jeff Beck [US: Epic PE 33409 (1975)]. He continues to work as a producer, heads the Facilities Division of Chrysalis Records, and currently operates AIR Studios on the Caribbean island of Montserrat. After a severe storm ravaged the island in 1989, Martin produced *After the Hurricane: Songs for Montserrat* [CD: Chrysalis F2 21750], a benefit for its citizens that features Paul McCartney. His memoir of the Beatle years, *All You Need is Ears,* was published in 1979.

Mike Smith: Liverpool music critic Tony Barrow, who also happened to write liner notes for Decca Records, helped Brian Epstein secure an audition for the band at the Cavern Club with Mike Smith, an assistant in Decca's artists and repertoire department. Smith was sufficiently impressed to follow up with a recorded audition at Decca's West Hampstead studios.

Smith acted as producer for the session, and guided the Fabs through a diverse set which included several songs that appeared nowhere else in the Beatle archive. In only a half hour the band recorded fifteen songs, including three Lennon-McCartney originals that were never released: "Love of the Loved," "Hello Little Girl," and "Like Dreamers Do."

Decca's artists and repertoire chief Dick Rowe had asked Smith to audition another group that day as well, Brian Poole and the Tremoloes from London. Smith's orders were to give a contract to only one group. The Tremoloes got the offer.

Phil Spector: The first recognized stylist among record producers, he pioneered the influential "wall of sound" during the early 1960s on such records as "River Deep, Mountain High" by Ike and Tina Turner, "Da Do Ron Ron" (Spector-Greenwich-Barry) by the Crystals, and "You've Lost That Lovin' Feelin" (Spector, Mann, Weil) by the Righteous Brothers.

The Beatles had been a fan of Spector's from the start; they performed his song "To Know Him Is to Love Him" (Spector) during their audition for Decca. Nor was he unaware of them, as he had produced a record called "Ringo I Love You" in 1964 for Bonnie Jo Mason (who later changed her name to Cher).

In early 1970, after working on John's single "Instant Karma," John and George recruited him to sift through the innumerable reels of tape left in the wake of the disastrous January 1969 *Get Back* sessions and produce an album.

Spector settled into the task of producing the new album, which included selecting new takes, remixing, overdubbing strings, brass, and chorus, and generally taking the album far afield of its original "live in the studio" concept. John, George, and Ringo appear to have been satisfied with the result. Paul, however, was horrified at Spector's heavy-handed treatment of the delicate "The Long and Winding Road," and tried to block the album's release. He was overruled, and in May 1970, *Let It Be* became the Beatles final release.

Spector's association with the ex-Beatles continued through several solo albums, including George's *All Things Must Pass* [CD: Parlophone/EMI CDP 7 46688/9 2 (1970)], *The Concert for Bangladesh* [US: Apple SCTX-3385 (1971)], and *Living in the Material World* [US: Apple SMAS-3410 (1973)], and John's *John Lennon/Plastic Ono Band* [CD: Parlophone 7 46770 2 (1970)], *Imagine* [CD: Parlophone/EMI 7 46641 2 (1971)], *Some Time in New York City* [CD: EMI CDP 7 46782/3 (1972)], and *Rock'n'Roll* [CD: Parlophone/EMI CDP 7 46707 2 (1975)].

During the making of *Rock 'n' Roll,* the producer's increasingly eccentric behavior—which culminated in his holding the tapes for a ransom of $200,000—brought his relationship with John to an end. Spector has remained out of the public eye since that time.

Legendary record producer Phil Spector.

The Beatles on Record

Even more than their legend and personalities, the Beatles were their music, and the only way to hear it today is on record. Recorded music assumes such a dizzying variety of forms that no discography can claim to encompass them all. In the mind of a Beatlemaniac, minute discrepancies assume elephantine proportions, leading to irrational (but thoroughly understandable) fetishism with regard to stereo and mono, label design, alternate mixes and fade-out times, picture disks, first pressings, nationality, cover art and inserts, standard and audiophile vinyl, and so on, ad infinitum.

What follows, then is an essential discography, rather than a complete one. In the case of official releases, the discography covers the basic Beatles oeuvre in the most accessible formats (LP/CDs, singles, and EPs), as well as some more obscure issues of special historical importance. (For American readers who may be unfamiliar with them, EPs are seven-inch (17.5-cm) disks played at the usual LP speed of 33⅓ rpm rather than 45 rpm, the proper speed for singles. For the most part issued only in Britain, EPs usually contain four songs.)-Also, a brief introduction to the wonderful world of acetates and other special issues points toward the most rewarding material in those areas.

For those seeking an even more complete picture of the Beatles' recorded output, a number of more comprehensive discographies are listed in chapter six, "The Beatles in Print," on p. 110.

Songwriting Credits

As became increasingly clear over the course of the group's active years, the Lennon-McCartney songwriting partnership was much of the time more a business arrangement than an actuality. John and Paul often did write music together, but just as often they didn't. In fact, they wrote together even less as their personal relationship wore thin. Still, with very few exceptions, their songs were credited to the pair for as long as the

Beatles lasted. Even John's first dramatic solo leap outside of the Beatles framework, his anthem "Give Peace a Chance," bore a Lennon-McCartney credit.

In the years following the Beatles' breakup, John and Paul's songwriting partnership became a popular interview topic, particularly with John, who clarified the authorship of many songs (although his accounts have been disputed by Paul and others). In addition, the differences between Lennon's and McCartney's styles have become sharply defined as a result of their solo recordings, improving the accuracy of the educated guess, although in some cases who wrote what is far from obvious. In many cases, the best indication is the lead voice on the recording: Paul sang his songs, John sang his songs, and both sang the songs they wrote together.

The primary authorship of most songs is, by now, relatively well established, except in rare cases where John's and Paul's accounts disagree ("In My Life" and "Eleanor Rigby"). In his book *Beatlesongs* (Simon & Schuster, 1989), William J. Dowlding collects relevant quotations from a variety of sources and goes so far as to assign a percentage of authorship to John, Paul, George, Ringo, and even Yoko ("Revolution 9") for each song. Although I have dispensed with the percentages, the credits appearing here agree with Dowlding for the most part. Paul's songs are credited to Lennon-**McCartney**, John's to **Lennon**-McCartney, and their collaborations to **Lennon**-**McCartney**. Where there is sufficient uncertainty, the credit reads Lennon-McCartney.

Of course, working together on the arrangements and performances, the songwriters were bound to contribute to one anothers' songs. A Lennon-**McCartney** song is rarely devoid of Lennon's influence, and vice versa. For instance, "I Saw Her Standing There" is, by John's admission, a McCartney song; still, the first couplet ran "She was just seventeen/Never been a beauty queen" until John suggested "You know what I mean" as a more intriguing alternative.

Numerous contributions were also made by non-Beatles, such as road manager Neil Aspinall's suggestion that four thousand holes in Blackburn, Lancashire were enough "to fill the Albert Hall" in "A Day in the Life" (**Lennon**-**McCartney**), or

George's mother's opinion that what the piggies, in whose lives something was lacking, really needed was "a damn good wacking" ("Piggies" [Harrison]). Neither Aspinall nor Mrs. Harrison received a songwriting credit.

Above: Fans at San Francisco's Cow Palace greet the Fab Four on the opening night of their first American tour, August 19, 1964. Opposite, top: The Beatles (circa 1965). Opposite, bottom: During the *Get Back* sessions, 1969.

Selected LP and CD Releases

Most people are familiar with the Beatles' repertoire from their official catalog on Parlophone (and Apple) in the U.K., and on Capitol (and Apple) in the U.S. The original U.S. LPs on Capitol, which were substantially different from those released by Parlophone in Britain, are now out of print and have been replaced by their British counterparts for current release in America. Early recordings were issued on a number of other labels as well, including Polydor, Swan, Tollie, MGM, and others. The latter are collectors' items today, but their material appears on "greatest hits" compilations and other reissues, so that virtually every significant Beatles release is in circulation in one form or another.

The following list is organized in chronological order according to U.S. release date, with U.S. vinyl issues listed first, followed by U.K. vinyl and finally CD issues (for which catalog numbers are, in most cases, consistent throughout the world). In order to convey a sense of the differences between the Beatles' American and British release schedules, records released in the U.K. but not in the U.S. are designated "No US release," and vice versa. Likewise, the unavailability of a title in CD format is indicated by "No CD release." No EPs or U.S. LPs have been issued in CD format.

Throughout the discographies, dates are represented as completely as possible. Dates for CD rereleases are not generally available, and therefore are omitted.

1961

Singles

TITLE	ARTIST	COMMENTS	LABEL/CATALOG NUMBER	RELEASE DATE
A: "My Bonnie (Lies Over the Ocean)" (Pratt) **B: "The Saints"** (trad., arr. Hines-Ward)	Tony Sheridan and the Beat Brothers		Germany only: Polydor 24 673 No CD release.	June 1961

Here is the first-ever Beatles record.

During their second trip to Hamburg—a good two years before Beatlemania broke out in Britain—the Beatles were approached by German producer Bert Kaempfert to back Tony Sheridan in recordings for the Polydor label. Kaempfert changed the group's name to the Beat Brothers because he feared that "Beatle" sounded a little too much like the Hamburg slang term "peedle," meaning penis.

The Polydor sessions, recorded on the stage of an elementary school, produced the following songs:

"My Bonnie (Lies Over the Ocean)" (Pratt)   Special intros to "My Bonnie," recorded in German and English, remain unreleased in the U.S.
"The Saints" (trad., arr. Hines-Ward)
"Why" (Sheridan-Compton)
"Nobody's Child" (trad., arr. Sheridan)
"If You Love Me, Baby" (Singleton-Hall)   Also titled "Take Out Some Insurance on Me, Baby."
"Sweet Georgia Brown" (Bernie-Pinkard-Casey)   The original vocal for "Sweet Georgia Brown" was rerecorded in 1963, and appears only on the 1962
"Cry for a Shadow" (Lennon-Harrison)   German EP.
"Ain't She Sweet" (Ager-Yellen)

Although Kaempfert's interest in the Beatles extended no further than as Sheridan's backup band, the pre-Fabs recorded the last two tracks without Sheridan. "Cry for a Shadow" is an instrumental parody of Britain's Cliff Richard and the Shadows, while "Ain't She Sweet" features John Lennon at the microphone, providing a well-recorded example of the Beatles' ensemble sound at the time.

Incidentally, this issue of "My Bonnie (Lies Over the Ocean)" is the only one that includes Sheridan's syrupy rubato introduction in German. The single was reported to have a value of $500 in 1977.

EPs

TITLE	ARTIST	COMMENTS	LABEL/CATALOG NUMBER	RELEASE DATE
My Bonnie	Tony Sheridan and the Beat Brothers		Germany only: Polydor (Catalog number not available) No CD release.	September 1961

- "My Bonnie (Lies Over the Ocean)" (Pratt)
- "Why" (Sheridan-Compton)
- "Cry for a Shadow" (Lennon-Harrison)
- "The Saints" (trad., arr. Sheridan)

1962

Singles

TITLE	ARTIST	COMMENTS	LABEL/CATALOG NUMBER	RELEASE DATE
A: "My Bonnie (Lies Over the Ocean)" (Pratt)	Tony Sheridan and the Beat Brothers		US: Decca 31382 UK: Polydor NH 66-833	April 23, 1962 January 5, 1962
B: "The Saints" (trad., arr. Hines-Ward)				

Decca, which had recently turned the Beatles down, issued the group's first record in the U.S., albeit under the name Beat Brothers. (Polydor, in the U.K., credited the recording to the Beatles.) Later, U.S. rights to this material were transferred to MGM, Atco, and many others which would exploit them far and wide for the next decade.

The U.K. issue of this single is the only version of "My Bonnie (Lies Over the Ocean)" to include Sheridan's rubato introduction in English.

TITLE	ARTIST	COMMENTS	LABEL/CATALOG NUMBER	RELEASE DATE
A: "Love Me Do" (Lennon-McCartney)	The Beatles	Ringo on drums.	No US release. UK: Parlophone R 4949	October 5, 1962
B: "P.S. I Love You" (Lennon-McCartney)		Andy White on drums.	No CD release.	

After an initial recording session on June 6, 1962, with Pete Best at the drum kit, producer George Martin mentioned to Brian Epstein that he wasn't happy with the drumming. While Best could play with the band on stage, he advised, a session player would be required for recordings.

When the time came to record the group's first single (on September 4, 1962), Martin was surprised to find that Best had been replaced by Ringo Starr. The rest of the band were even more surprised when Martin, after the session, informed them that they would have to remake the song with yet another drummer. One week later, a humiliated Ringo shook the tambourine, and then a pair of maracas, as session man Andy White played his drum part on both "Love Me Do" and "P.S. I Love You."

(Ringo has explained that Martin formed the impression that he couldn't keep time upon hearing him rehearse "Love Me Do" because he was playing both the drum and the percussion parts at once. Regardless, a quick listen confirms that the Andy White recording is the better, for reasons that aren't confined to the drumming. It appears that previous to the September 4 session, John had always sung "Love me do" at the end of the verse, dropping "do" in order to perform the song's signature harmonica lick: "Love me—*waaah*." Martin found this unacceptable, and demanded that Paul sing the line instead; thus, McCartney suddenly found himself with an a cappella vocal solo on the band's first single. His frayed nerves are quite audible in the recording.)

For reasons that may boil down to simple confusion, it was Ringo's take of "Love Me Do" that made it onto the Beatles' first single. Thereafter, however, the Andy White take has been used, and has appeared on EP, LP, and reissues of the single. Today, Ringo's performance is most readily available on the compilation *Past Masters Volume One*.

EPs

TITLE	ARTIST	COMMENTS	LABEL/CATALOG NUMBER	RELEASE DATE
Ya-Ya	Tony Sheridan and the Beat Brothers		Germany only: Polydor 21485 No CD release.	October 1962

- "Ya-Ya (Part 1)" (Robinson-Dorsey)
- "Ya-Ya (Part 2)" (Robinson-Dorsey)
- "Sweet Georgia Brown" (Bernie-Pinkard-Casey)   Original vocal.
- "Skinny Minny"

The Beatles appear only on "Sweet Georgia Brown," which is unique in this issue insofar as it includes the original lead vocal by Tony Sheridan. He re-recorded the vocal for later releases.

1963

LPs & CDs

TITLE	ARTIST	COMMENTS	LABEL/CATALOG NUMBER	RELEASE DATE
Please Please Me			No US release. UK: Parlophone PCS 3042 CD: Parlophone CDP 7 46435-2	March 22, 1963

- "I Saw Her Standing There" (Lennon-**McCartney**)
- "Misery" (**Lennon-McCartney**)
- "Anna (Go to Him)" (Alexander)
- "Chains" (Goffin-King)
- "Boys" (Dixon-Farrell)
- "Ask Me Why" (**Lennon**-McCartney)
- "Please Please Me" (**Lennon**-McCartney)   Parlophone/Capitol LP version without vocal flub.
- "Love Me Do" (**Lennon-McCartney**)   Andy White on drums.
- "P.S. I Love You" (Lennon-**McCartney**)   Andy White on drums.
- "Baby, It's You" (David-Bacharach-Williams)
- "Do You Want to Know a Secret" (**Lennon**-McCartney)
- "A Taste of Honey" (Marlow-Scott)
- "There's a Place" (**Lennon**-McCartney)
- "Twist and Shout" (Medley-Russell)

George Martin had considered recording the Beatles' first album live at the Cavern Club. When that venue's acoustics proved untenable, he opted for EMI's Abbey Road Studios. On February 11, 1963, in one thirteen-hour session, the Beatles raced the clock to record the selection of Cavern favorites that made up the bulk of *Please Please Me*.

TITLE	ARTIST	COMMENTS	LABEL/CATALOG NUMBER	RELEASE DATE

Introducing the Beatles

US: Vee Jay VJLP 1062

No UK release.

No CD release.

July 22, 1963

- "I Saw Her Standing There" (Lennon-**McCartney**)
- "Misery" (**Lennon-McCartney**)
- "Anna (Go to Him)" (Alexander)
- "Chains" (Goffin-King)
- "Boys" (Dixon-Farrell)
- "Love Me Do" (**Lennon-McCartney**)   Andy White on drums.
- "P.S. I Love You" (Lennon-**McCartney**)
- "Baby, It's You" (David-Bacharach-Williams)
- "Do You Want to Know a Secret" (**Lennon**-McCartney)
- "A Taste of Honey" (Marlow-Scott)
- "There's a Place" (**Lennon**-McCartney)
- "Twist and Shout" (Medley-Russell)

A January 27, 1964, reissue of this album, bearing the same catalog number, exchanged "Ask Me Why" (**Lennon**-McCartney) and "Please Please Me" (**Lennon**-McCartney) [Vee Jay/single/EP version with John's vocal flub] for "Love Me Do" and "P.S. I Love You."

With the Beatles

No US release.

UK: Parlophone PCS 3045

CD: Parlophone CDP 7 46436 2

November 22, 1963

- "It Won't Be Long" (**Lennon**-McCartney)
- "All I've Got to Do" (**Lennon**-McCartney)
- "All My Loving" (Lennon-**McCartney**)
- "Don't Bother Me" (Harrison)
- "Little Child" (**Lennon-McCartney**)
- "Till There Was You" (Willson)
- "Please Mr. Postman" (Holland-Bateman-Gordy)
- "Roll Over Beethoven" (Berry)
- "Hold Me Tight" (**Lennon-McCartney**)
- "You Really Got a Hold on Me" (Robinson)
- "I Wanna Be Your Man" (**Lennon-McCartney**)
- "(There's a) Devil in Her Heart" (Drapkin)
- "Not a Second Time" (**Lennon**-McCartney)
- "Money (That's What I Want)" (Gordy-Bradford)

*We wrote for our market. We knew that if we wrote a song called "Thank You Girl"
that a lot of the girls who wrote us fan letters would take it as a genuine thank-you. So
a lot of our songs—"From Me to You" is another—were directly addressed to the
fans.*

—Paul McCartney, *The Beatles: Recording Sessions* **by Mark Lewisohn, 1988**

Singles

TITLE	ARTIST	COMMENTS	LABEL/CATALOG NUMBER	RELEASE DATE
A: "Please Please Me" (**Lennon**-McCartney) B: "Ask Me Why" (**Lennon**-McCartney)		Vee Jay/single/EP version with John's vocal flub.	US: Vee Jay VJ 498 UK: Parlophone R 4983 CD: EMI C3-44279	February 25, 1963 January 11, 1963

When the Beatles' second single, "Please Please Me," reached Number One in the U.K. charts, George Martin offered it to Capitol, the U.S. subsidiary of EMI (Parlophone's mother company). Capitol declined. In fact, with each new single, Martin returned to Capitol, and each time the answer was the same: The Beatles' sound would never sell in the American market. (One of the Capitol executives involved in the decision making at the time recently revealed that it was the presence of John Lennon's harmonica that made the Fabs' sound unsuitable.)

Thus, the first few Parlophone singles to be released in the U.S. came out on two small American labels, Vee Jay and Swan. Just as Capitol's executives had predicted, neither had any success.

When the Beatles finally hit it big in the U.S. one year later, Vee Jay was ready with a reissue of "Please Please Me"; the company continued to reissue their precious Beatle recordings well into the next decade.

In Vee Jay's version of "Please Please Me," as well as that on U.K. singles and EPs, John flubs the vocal. A different take was selected for Parlophone, as well as for Capitol LPs and CDs.

TITLE	ARTIST	COMMENTS	LABEL/CATALOG NUMBER	RELEASE DATE
A: "From Me to You" (**Lennon**-**McCartney**) B: "Thank You Girl" (**Lennon**-**McCartney**)			US: Vee Jay VJ 522 UK: Parlophone R 5015 CD: EMI C3-44280	May 27, 1963 April 12, 1963
A: "She Loves You" (**Lennon**-**McCartney**) B: "I'll Get You" (**Lennon**-**McCartney**)			US: Swan 4152 UK: Parlophone R 5055 CD: EMI C3-44281	September 16, 1963 August 30, 1963
A: "I Want to Hold Your Hand" (**Lennon**-**McCartney**) B: "This Boy" (**Lennon**-McCartney)			No US release. UK: Parlophone R 5084 CD: EMI C3-44304	November 29, 1963

EPs

TITLE	ARTIST	COMMENTS	LABEL/CATALOG NUMBER	RELEASE DATE
Twist and Shout			No US release. UK: Parlophone GEP 8882 No CD release.	July 12, 1963

- "Twist and Shout" (Medley-Russell)
- "A Taste of Honey" (Marlow-Scott)
- "Do You Want to Know a Secret?" (**Lennon**-McCartney)
- "There's a Place" (**Lennon**-McCartney)

TITLE	ARTIST	COMMENTS	LABEL/CATALOG NUMBER	RELEASE DATE

The Beatles' Hits

No US release.
UK: Parlophone GEP 8880
No CD release.

September 6, 1963

- "From Me to You" (**Lennon-McCartney**)
- "Thank You Girl" (**Lennon-McCartney**)
- "Please Please Me" (**Lennon**-McCartney)   Vee Jay/single/EP version with John's vocal flub.
- "Love Me Do" (**Lennon-McCartney**)

The Beatles (No. 1)

No US release.
UK: Parlophone GEP 8883
No CD release.

November 1, 1963

- "I Saw Her Standing There" (Lennon-**McCartney**)
- "Misery" (**Lennon-McCartney**)
- "Anna (Go to Him)" (Alexander)
- "Chains" (Goffin-King)

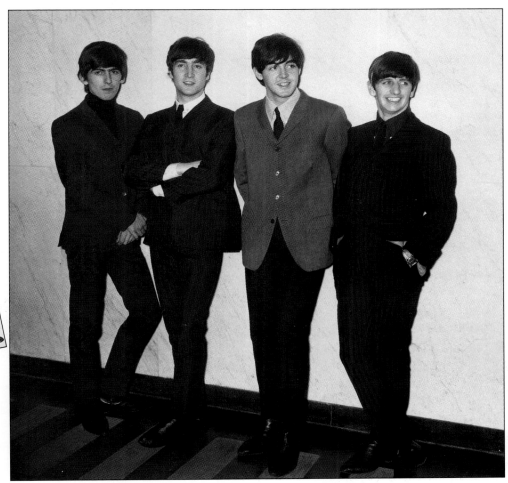

George, John, Paul, and Ringo (circa 1964).

1964

LPs & CDs

TITLE	ARTIST	COMMENTS	LABEL/CATALOG NUMBER	RELEASE DATE

Meet the Beatles!

US: Capitol ST 2047
No UK release.
No CD release.

January 20, 1964

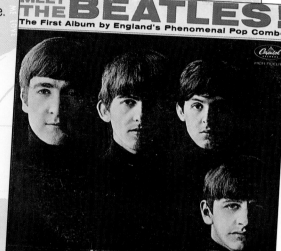

- "I Want to Hold Your Hand" (**Lennon**-**McCartney**)
- "I Saw Her Standing There" (Lennon-**McCartney**)
- "This Boy" (**Lennon**-McCartney)
- "It Won't Be Long" (**Lennon**-McCartney)
- "All I've Got to Do" (**Lennon**-McCartney)
- "All My Loving" (Lennon-**McCartney**)
- "Don't Bother Me" (Harrison)
- "Little Child" (**Lennon**-McCartney)
- "Till There Was You" (Willson)
- "Hold Me Tight" (**Lennon**-McCartney)
- "I Wanna Be Your Man" (**Lennon**-**McCartney**)
- "Not a Second Time" (**Lennon**-McCartney)

The first Beatle album on Capitol, and the first example of Capitol's strategy for squeezing extra records out of the Beatles output.

Meet the Beatles is basically the U.K. album *With the Beatles*, but with a few wrinkles: First of all, there are twelve songs rather than fourteen—an automatic saving of the cost of producing two fewer songs. "I Saw Her Standing There" is a holdover from the older U.K. release *Please Please Me*. "I Want to Hold Your Hand" and "This Boy" come from a U.K. single, neither having appeared on a U.K. LP due to the British policy of avoiding such overlap.

Thus, the album includes only nine of *With the Beatles'* fourteen songs, leaving five—not to mention forthcoming U.K. single and EP tracks—available for Capitol's next LP release.

The Beatles' Second Album

US: Capitol ST 2080
No UK release.
No CD release.

April 10, 1964

- "Roll Over Beethoven" (Berry)
- "Thank You Girl" (**Lennon**-**McCartney**)
- "You Really Got a Hold on Me" (Robinson)
- "(There's a) Devil in Her Heart" (Drapkin)
- "Money (That's What I Want)" (Gordy-Bradford)   LP take.
- "You Can't Do That" (**Lennon**-McCartney)
- "Long Tall Sally" (Johnson-Penniman-Blackwell)
- "I Call Your Name" (**Lennon**-McCartney)
- "Please Mr. Postman" (Holland-Bateman-Gordy)
- "I'll Get You" (**Lennon**-**McCartney**)
- "She Loves You" (**Lennon**-**McCartney**)

TITLE	ARTIST	COMMENTS	LABEL/CATALOG NUMBER	RELEASE DATE

The Beatles' First
(CD title: ***Early Tapes
of the Beatles***)

Tony Sheridan
and the Beatles

No US release.
UK: Polydor 236-201
CD: Polydor 823 701-2

June 19, 1964

- "Ain't She Sweet" (Ager-Yellen)
- "Cry For a Shadow" (Lennon-Harrison)
- "My Bonnie" (trad., arr. Sheridan)
- "If You Love Me, Baby" (Singleton-Hall)
- "Sweet Georgia Brown" (Bernie-Pinkard-Casey)   Revised vocal.
- "The Saints" (trad., arr. Hines-Ward)
- "Why" (Sheridan-Compton)
- "Nobody's Child" (trad., arr. Sheridan)
- Plus other titles recorded by Sheridan without the Beatles.

The initial LP release of the Sheridan sessions in the U.K. occurred about one month earlier, in May 1964, when Polydor packaged four of the tracks with songs by bands which, bearing names like the Jacques Denjean Orchestra, couldn't possibly have been beat groups. This album collected, for the first time, the entire Sheridan/Beatles archive.

A Hard Day's Night
(soundtrack)

US: United Artists UAS 6366
UK: Parlophone PCS 3058
CD: Parlophone CDP 7 46437-2

June 26, 1964
July 10, 1964

- "A Hard Day's Night" (**Lennon**-McCartney)
- "I Should Have Known Better" (**Lennon**-McCartney)
- "If I Fell" (**Lennon**-McCartney)
- "I'm Happy Just to Dance with You" (**Lennon**-McCartney)
- "And I Love Her" (Lennon-**McCartney**)
- "Tell Me Why" (**Lennon**-McCartney)
- "Can't Buy Me Love" (Lennon-**McCartney**)
- "Anytime at All" (**Lennon**-McCartney)   UK only.
- "I'll Cry Instead" (**Lennon**-McCartney)   The U.S. soundtrack and single include an extra verse.
- "Things We Said Today" (Lennon-**McCartney**)   UK only.
- "When I Get Home" (**Lennon**-McCartney)   UK only.
- "You Can't Do That" (**Lennon**-McCartney)   UK only.
- "I'll Be Back" (**Lennon**-McCartney)   UK only.
- Plus additional music arranged and performed by
  George Martin & Orchestra   US only.

United Artist's deal with the Beatles gave the company U.S. rights to the soundtrack album for the Fab Four's first motion picture. United Artists interspersed new Beatle songs with excerpts from the film's score by George Martin. Parlophone's U.K. *A Hard Day's Night*, on the other hand, delivered songs from the movie on one side and a batch of new, unrelated Beatles songs on the other.

TITLE	ARTIST	COMMENTS	LABEL/CATALOG NUMBER	RELEASE DATE

Something New

US: Capitol ST 2108

No UK release.

No CD release.

July 20, 1964

- "I'll Cry Instead" (**Lennon**-McCartney)   Usual version, lacking extra verse.
- "Things We Said Today" (Lennon-**McCartney**)
- "Anytime at All" (**Lennon**-McCartney)
- "When I Get Home" (**Lennon**-McCartney)
- "Slow Down" (Williams)
- "Matchbox" (trad., arr. Perkins)
- "Tell Me Why" (**Lennon**-McCartney)
- "And I Love Her" (Lennon-**McCartney**)
- "I'm Happy Just to Dance with You" (**Lennon**-McCartney)
- "If I Fell" (**Lennon**-McCartney)
- "Komm, Gib Mir Deine Hand" (**Lennon**-**McCartney**-Nicolas-Hellmer)

The Beatles Story

US: Capitol STBO 2222

No UK release.

No CD release.

November 23, 1964

(See "Spoken-Word Releases," p. 84.)

Beatles for Sale

No US release.

UK: Parlophone PCS 3062

CD: Parlophone CDP 7 46438-2

December 4, 1964

- "No Reply" (**Lennon**-McCartney)
- "I'm a Loser" (**Lennon**-McCartney)
- "Baby's in Black" (**Lennon**-**McCartney**)
- "Rock and Roll Music" (Berry)
- "I'll Follow the Sun" (Lennon-**McCartney**)
- "Mr. Moonlight" (Johnson)
- "Kansas City"/"Hey Hey Hey Hey!" (Leiber-Stoller/Penniman)
- "Eight Days a Week" (**Lennon**-**McCartney**)
- "Words of Love" (Holly)
- "Honey Don't" (Perkins)
- "Every Little Thing" (Lennon-**McCartney**)
- "I Don't Want to Spoil the Party" (**Lennon**-McCartney)
- "What You're Doing" (Lennon-**McCartney**)
- "Everybody's Trying to Be My Baby" (Perkins)

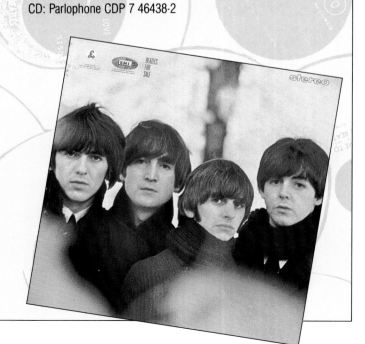

TITLE	ARTIST	COMMENTS	LABEL/CATALOG NUMBER	RELEASE DATE

The Beatles '65

US: Capitol ST 2228

No UK release.

No CD release.

December 15, 1964

- "No Reply" (**Lennon**-McCartney)
- "I'm a Loser" (**Lennon**-McCartney)
- "Baby's in Black" (**Lennon-McCartney**)
- "Rock and Roll Music" (Berry)
- "I'll Follow the Sun" (Lennon-**McCartney**)
- "Mr. Moonlight" (Johnson)
- "Honey Don't" (Perkins)
- "I'll Be Back" (**Lennon**-McCartney)
- "She's a Woman" (Lennon-**McCartney**)
- "I Feel Fine" (**Lennon**-McCartney)
- "Everybody's Trying to Be My Baby" (Perkins)

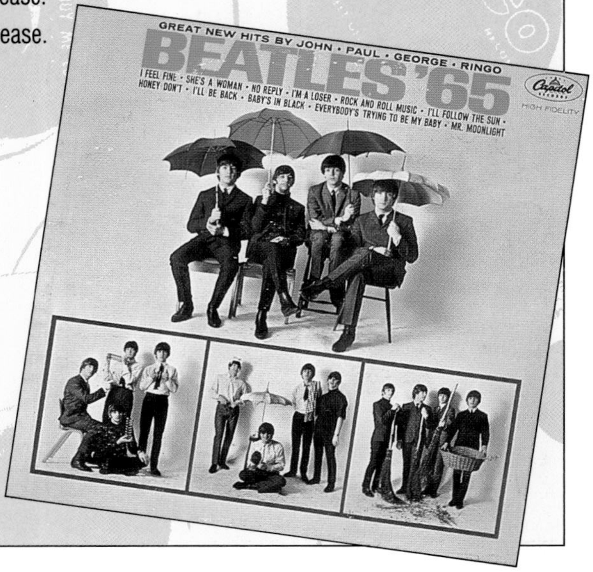

Singles

TITLE	ARTIST	COMMENTS	LABEL/CATALOG NUMBER	RELEASE DATE

A: "I Want to Hold Your Hand"
(**Lennon**-**McCartney**)
B: "I Saw Her Standing There"
(Lennon-**McCartney**)

US: Capitol 5112

No UK release.

No CD release.

January 13, 1964

Capitol finally came around after DJs began playing imported copies of the Beatles' Parlophone single, "I Want to Hold Your Hand"/"This Boy." The U.S. release, buttressed by a massive publicity campaign, became an instant sensation in America—just in time for the Beatles' first appearance on *The Ed Sullivan Show*.

A: "Twist and Shout"
(Medley-Russell)
B: "There's a Place"
(**Lennon**-McCartney)

US: Tollie 9001

No UK release.

No CD release.

March 2, 1964

This single, on an obscure American label, marks the only U.S. appearance of "There's a Place" until its reissue on *Rarities* in 1980. This song is the earliest example of the deeply personal approach that later became the hallmark of John Lennon's style.

A: "Can't Buy Me Love"
(Lennon-**McCartney**)
B: "You Can't Do That"
(**Lennon**-McCartney)

US: Capitol 5150
UK: Parlophone R 5114
CD: EMI C3-44305

March 16, 1964
March 20, 1964

TITLE	ARTIST	COMMENTS	LABEL/CATALOG NUMBER	RELEASE DATE
A: "Do You Want to Know a Secret?" (**Lennon**-McCartney) B: "Thank You Girl" (**Lennon**-**McCartney**)			US: Vee Jay VJ 587 No UK release. No CD release.	March 23, 1964
A: "Love Me Do" (**Lennon**-McCartney) B: "P.S. I Love You" (Lennon-**McCartney**)		Andy White on drums.	US: Tollie 9008 No UK release. CD: EMI C3-44278	April 27, 1964
A: "Sie Leibt Dich" (**Lennon**-**McCartney**- Nicolas-Montague) B: "I'll Get You" (**Lennon**-**McCartney**)			US: Swan 4182 No UK release. No CD release.	May 21, 1964

A rare and difficult-to-explain U.S. release of the German-language "She Loves You."

TITLE	ARTIST	COMMENTS	LABEL/CATALOG NUMBER	RELEASE DATE
A: "Komm, Gib Mir Deine Hand" (**Lennon**-**McCartney**- Nicolas-Hellmer) B: "Sie Leibt Dich" (**Lennon**-**McCartney**- Nicolas-Montague)			Germany only: Odeon 22671 No CD release.	March 5, 1964

EMI representatives in Germany insisted that the Beatles wouldn't be successful in their country unless they sang in the native tongue. This seemed absurd to the Beatles, who had already been successful when singing in English to the German patrons of Hamburg's nightclubs. George Martin, however, recognized the importance of supporting foreign markets and persuaded the Fabs to rerecord their two biggest hits.

On the morning of the recording session, the group failed to arrive at the studio. After an hour's wait, Martin phoned their hotel room, but they wouldn't take the call. Finally, he drove to the hotel and barged into their room. "Beatles ran in all directions," he recalls in *All You Need is Ears*, "hiding behind sofas, cushions, the piano—anything that gave them cover."

Martin gave the boys a scolding and rebooked the session, and the next day, January 29, 1964, they recorded the German tracks. When he heard the results, though, he saw their point. " 'Sie leibt dich, ja, ja, ja,' " he commented, "sounded just like the sort of send-up Peter Sellers would have done."

TITLE	ARTIST	COMMENTS	LABEL/CATALOG NUMBER	RELEASE DATE
A: "Ain't She Sweet" (Ager-Yellen) B: "If You Love Me, Baby" (Singleton-Hall)	The Beatles with Tony Sheridan		No US release. UK: Polydor NH 52-317 No CD release.	May 29, 1964

This marks the first release anywhere of the Beatles' "Ain't She Sweet," a rather lackluster arrangement redeemed by John's energetic vocal, recorded during the 1961 Tony Sheridan sessions. It remains the earliest recording of the group to be officially released.

TITLE	ARTIST	COMMENTS	LABEL/CATALOG NUMBER	RELEASE DATE
A: "A Hard Day's Night" (**Lennon**-McCartney) B: "Things We Said Today" (Lennon-**McCartney**)			No US release. UK: Parlophone R 5160 CD: EMI C3-44306	July 10, 1964
A: "A Hard Day's Night" (**Lennon**-McCartney) B: "I Should Have Known Better" (**Lennon**-McCartney)			US: Capitol 5222 No UK release. No CD release.	July 13, 1964
A: "I'll Cry Instead" (**Lennon**-McCartney) B: "I'm Happy Just to Dance with You" (**Lennon**-McCartney)		US soundtrack/single version, including an extra verse.	US: Capitol 5234 No UK release. No CD release.	July 20, 1964
A: "And I Love Her" (Lennon-**McCartney**) B: "If I Fell" (**Lennon**-McCartney)			US: Capitol 5235 No UK release. No CD release.	July 20, 1964
A: "Slow Down" (Williams) B: "Matchbox" (trad., arr. Perkins)			US: Capitol 5255 No UK release. No CD release.	August 24, 1964
A: "I Feel Fine" (**Lennon**-McCartney) B: "She's a Woman" (Lennon-**McCartney**)			US: Capitol 5327 UK: Parlophone R 5200 CD: EMI C3-44321	November 23, 1964 November 27, 1964

EPs

TITLE	ARTIST	COMMENTS	LABEL/CATALOG NUMBER	RELEASE DATE

All My Loving

No US release.
UK: Parlophone GEP 8891
No CD release.

February 7, 1964

- "All My Loving" (Lennon-**McCartney**)
- "Ask Me Why" (**Lennon**-McCartney)
- "Money (That's What I Want)" (Gordy-Bradford)   EP take different from single and LP.
- "P.S. I Love You" (Lennon-**McCartney**)

**Souvenir of Their Visit
to America**

US: Vee Jay EP 1-903
No UK release.
No CD release.

March 23, 1964

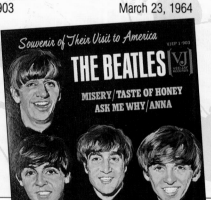

- "Misery" (**Lennon-McCartney**)
- "A Taste of Honey" (Marlow-Scott)
- "Ask Me Why" (**Lennon**-McCartney)
- "Anna" (Alexander)

The only Beatle EP issued on Vee Jay, and one of the only three issued in the U.S.

Four by the Beatles

US: Capitol EAP 2121
No UK release.
No CD release.

May 11, 1964

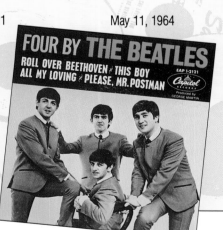

- "Roll Over Beethoven" (Berry)
- "All My Loving" (Lennon-**McCartney**)
- "This Boy" (**Lennon**-McCartney)
- "Please Mr. Postman" (Holland-Bateman-Gordy)

Capitol's short-lived experiment with the EP format in America.

Long Tall Sally

No US release.
UK: Parlophone GEP 8913
No CD release.

June 19, 1964

- "Long Tall Sally" (Johnson-Penniman-Blackwell)
- "I Call Your Name" (**Lennon**-McCartney)
- "Slow Down" (Williams)
- "Matchbox" (trad., arr. Perkins)

A scene from the U.K. television special *Around the Beatles,* 1964.

TITLE	ARTIST	COMMENTS	LABEL/CATALOG NUMBER	RELEASE DATE
Extracts from the Film A Hard Day's Night			No US release. UK: Parlophone GEP 8920 No CD release.	November 4, 1964

- "I Should Have Known Better" (**Lennon**-McCartney)
- "If I Fell" (**Lennon**-McCartney)
- "Tell Me Why" (**Lennon**-McCartney)
- "And I Love Her" (Lennon-**McCartney**)

TITLE	ARTIST	COMMENTS	LABEL/CATALOG NUMBER	RELEASE DATE
Extracts from the Album A Hard Day's Night			No US release. UK: Parlophone GEP 8924 No CD release.	November 6, 1964

- "Anytime at All" (**Lennon**-McCartney)
- "I'll Cry Instead" (**Lennon**-McCartney)   The usual version, lacking extra verse.
- "Things We Said Today" (Lennon-**McCartney**)
- "When I Get Home" (**Lennon**-McCartney)

1965

LPs & CDs

TITLE	ARTIST	COMMENTS	LABEL/CATALOG NUMBER	RELEASE DATE

The Early Beatles

US: Capitol ST 2309

No UK release.

No CD release.

March 22, 1965

Capitol's rehash of tracks originally issued by Vee Jay as *Introducing the Beatles*.

Beatles VI

US: Capitol ST 2358

No UK release.

No CD release.

June 14, 1965

- "Kansas City"/"Hey Hey Hey Hey!" (Leiber-Stoller/Penniman)
- "Eight Days a Week" (**Lennon**-**McCartney**)
- "You Like Me Too Much" (Harrison)
- "Bad Boy" (Williams)
- "I Don't Want to Spoil the Party" (**Lennon**-McCartney)
- "Words of Love" (Holly)
- "What You're Doing" (Lennon-**McCartney**)
- "Yes It Is" (**Lennon**-McCartney)
- "Dizzy Miss Lizzie" (Williams)
- "Tell Me What You See" (Lennon-**McCartney**)
- "Every Little Thing" (Lennon-**McCartney**)

The Beatles in 1964 with British Prime Minister Harold Wilson—the same "Mr. Wilson" mentioned in George's "Tax Man."

TITLE	ARTIST	COMMENTS	LABEL/CATALOG NUMBER	RELEASE DATE

Help!
(soundtrack)

US: Capitol SMAS 2386
UK: Parlophone PCS 3071
CD: Parlophone CDP 7 46439 2

August 13, 1965
August 6, 1965

- "Help!" (**Lennon**-McCartney) — LP version, different lead vocal than single.
- "The Night Before" (Lennon-**McCartney**)
- "You've Got to Hide Your Love Away" (**Lennon**-McCartney)
- "I Need You" (Harrison)
- "Another Girl" (Lennon-**McCartney**)
- "You're Gonna Lose That Girl" (**Lennon**-McCartney)
- "Ticket to Ride" (**Lennon**-McCartney)
- "Act Naturally" (Russell-Morrison) — UK only.
- "It's Only Love" (**Lennon**-McCartney) — UK only.
- "You Like Me Too Much" (Harrison) — UK only.
- "Tell Me What You See" (Lennon-**McCartney**) — UK only.
- "I've Just Seen a Face" (Lennon-**McCartney**) — UK only.
- "Yesterday" (Lennon-**McCartney**)
- "Dizzy Miss Lizzie" (Williams) — UK only.
- Plus additional titles arranged and performed by George Martin & Orchestra — US only.

As with *A Hard Day's Night,* the U.S. version of the *Help!* soundtrack interspersed Beatle performances with orchestral arrangements by George Martin, while the U.K. package delivered a full album's worth of new Beatle songs.

(See Chapter five, "The Beatles on Film: Feature Films," p. 104)

Rubber Soul

US: Capitol ST 2442
UK: Parlophone PCS 3075
CD: Parlophone CDP 7 46440 2

December 6, 1965
December 3, 1965

- "Drive My Car" (**Lennon**-**McCartney**) — UK only.
- "Norwegian Wood (This Bird Has Flown)" (**Lennon**-McCartney)
- "You Won't See Me" (Lennon-**McCartney**)
- "Nowhere Man" (**Lennon**-McCartney) — UK only.
- "Think for Yourself" (Harrison)
- "The Word" (**Lennon**-**McCartney**)
- "Michelle" (**Lennon**-**McCartney**)
- "What Goes On?" (Lennon-McCartney-Starkey) — UK only.
- "Girl" (**Lennon**-McCartney)
- "I'm Looking Through You" (Lennon-**McCartney**)
- "In My Life" (Lennon-McCartney)
- "Wait" (**Lennon**-**McCartney**)
- "If I Needed Someone" (Harrison) — UK only.
- "Run for Your Life" (**Lennon**-McCartney)
- "I've Just Seen a Face" (Lennon-**McCartney**) — US only.
- "It's Only Love" (**Lennon**-McCartney) — US only.

Singles

TITLE	ARTIST	COMMENTS	LABEL/CATALOG NUMBER	RELEASE DATE
A: "If I Fell" (**Lennon**-McCartney) B: "Tell Me Why" (**Lennon**-McCartney)			No US release. UK: Parlophone DP 562 CD: Information not available.	January 19, 1965
A: "Eight Days a Week" (**Lennon-McCartney**) B: "I Don't Want to Spoil the Party" (**Lennon**-McCartney)			US: Capitol 5371 No UK release. No CD release.	February 15, 1965
A: "Ticket to Ride" (**Lennon**-McCartney) B: "Yes It Is" (**Lennon**-McCartney)			US: Capitol 5407 UK: Parlophone R 5265 CD: EMI C3-44307	April 19, 1965 April 9, 1965
A: "Help!" (**Lennon**-McCartney) B: "I'm Down" (Lennon-**McCartney**)		Single version, different lead vocal from LP.	US: Capitol 5476 UK: Parlophone R 5305 CD: Information not available.	19, 1965 ?3, 1965
A: "Yesterday" (Lennon-**McCartney**) B: "Act Naturally" (Russell-Morrison)			US: Capitol 5498 No UK release. No CD release.	September 13, 1965
A: "We Can Work It Out" (**Lennon-McCartney**) B: "Day Tripper" (**Lennon**-McCartney)			US: Capitol 5555 UK: Parlophone R 5389 CD: EMI CD3R-5389	December 6, 1965 December 3, 1965

EPs

TITLE	ARTIST	COMMENTS	LABEL/CATALOG NUMBER	RELEASE DATE

Beatles for Sale

No US release.
UK: Parlophone GEP 8931 — April 6, 1964
No CD release.

- "No Reply" (**Lennon**-McCartney)
- "I'm a Loser" (**Lennon**-McCartney)
- "Rock and Roll Music" (Berry)
- "Eight Days a Week" (**Lennon-McCartney**)

Beatles for Sale (No. 2)

No US release.
UK: Parlophone GEP 8938 — June 4, 1964
No CD release.

- "I'll Follow the Sun" (Lennon-**McCartney**)
- "Baby's in Black" (**Lennon-McCartney**)
- "Words of Love" (Holly)
- "I Don't Want to Spoil the Party" (**Lennon**-McCartney)

4 by the Beatles

US: Capitol R 5365 — February 1, 1965
No UK release.
No CD release.

- "Honey Don't" (Perkins)
- "I'm a Loser" (**Lennon**-McCartney)
- "Mr. Moonlight" (Johnson)
- "Everybody's Trying to Be My Baby" (Perkins)

Capitol's second, and final, Beatles EP.

Our best work was never recorded. We were performers in Liverpool, Hamburg and other dance halls. What we generated was fantastic when we played straight rock, and there was nobody to touch us in Britain. As soon as we made it, we made it, but the edges were knocked off. . . . The music was dead before we even went on the theater tour of Britain.

—John Lennon, *Rolling Stone*, January 7/February 4, 1971, reprinted in *The Ballad of John and Yoko*, Jonathan Cott and Christine Doudna, eds., 1982

TITLE	ARTIST	COMMENTS	LABEL/CATALOG NUMBER	RELEASE DATE

The Beatles' Million Sellers

(also issued as

Beatles' Golden

Discs)

- "She Loves You" (**Lennon-McCartney**)
- "I Want to Hold Your Hand" (**Lennon-McCartney**)
- "Can't Buy Me Love" (Lennon-**McCartney**)
- "I Feel Fine" (**Lennon**-McCartney)

		No US release.		
		UK: Parlophone GEP 8946		December 6, 1965
		No CD release.		

1966

LPs & CDs

TITLE	ARTIST	COMMENTS	LABEL/CATALOG NUMBER	RELEASE DATE

Yesterday . . . And

   Today

- "Drive My Car" (**Lennon-McCartney**)
- "I'm Only Sleeping" (**Lennon**-McCartney)
- "Nowhere Man" (**Lennon**-McCartney)
- "Dr. Robert" (**Lennon-McCartney**)
- "Yesterday" (Lennon-**McCartney**)
- "Act Naturally" (Russell-Morrison)
- "And Your Bird Can Sing" (**Lennon**-McCartney)
- "If I Needed Someone" (Harrison)
- "We Can Work It Out" (**Lennon-McCartney**)
- "What Goes On?" (Lennon-McCartney-Starkey)
- "Day Tripper" (**Lennon**-McCartney)

		US: Capitol ST 2553		June 20, 1966
		No UK release.		
		No CD release.		

By mid-1966 such was the Beatles' command of the marketplace that—for a short moment—their authority was unquestioned. Thus, it was only with the slightest flinch that Capitol printed 750,000 copies of the original *Yesterday... And Today* cover. It depicted the Fab Four smiling wryly in white butcher smocks, their laps and shoulders strewn with mutilated toy dolls and slabs of raw meat.

This album cover was the first clear indication that the Beatles had had enough of superstardom, and it was not well received by a shocked and uncomprehending public. Shipment of the LP came to an abrupt halt as Capitol employees scrambled to paste an innocuous photo over the offending cover, making the first edition of *Yesterday... And Today* an instant collector's item.

Today, a mint-condition butcher sleeve can fetch as much as $2,000.

TITLE	ARTIST	COMMENTS	LABEL/CATALOG NUMBER	RELEASE DATE

Revolver

US: Capitol ST 2576 — August 8, 1966
UK: Parlophone PCS 7009 — August 5, 1966
CD: Parlophone CDP 7 46441 2

- "Taxman" (Harrison)
- "Eleanor Rigby" (Lennon-**McCartney**)
- "I'm Only Sleeping" (**Lennon**-McCartney) — UK only.
- "Love You Too" (Harrison)
- "Here, There, and Everywhere" (Lennon-**McCartney**)
- "Yellow Submarine" (Lennon-**McCartney**)
- "She Said She Said" (**Lennon**-McCartney)
- "Good Day Sunshine" (Lennon-**McCartney**)
- "And Your Bird Can Sing" (**Lennon**-McCartney) — UK only.
- "For No One" (Lennon-**McCartney**)
- "Dr. Robert" (**Lennon**-**McCartney**) — UK only.
- "I Want to Tell You" (Harrison)
- "Got to Get You into My Life" (Lennon-**McCartney**)
- "Tomorrow Never Knows" (**Lennon**-McCartney)

This release clearly marks the arrival of a new era for the Beatles. The stylistic range of the songs is extraordinary, from the backbeat rock'n'roll of "Taxman" to the balladry of "Here, There, and Everywhere," from the dead-on pop sensibility of "Got to Get You into My Life" to the children's rhyme of "Yellow Submarine." The most arresting track, "Tomorrow Never Knows," with its interjections of unidentifiable sounds, showed that the Beatles had a new awareness of the recording studio as a musical instrument, and of the recording itself as the only viable way of presenting their compositions. Popular music would never again be the same.

A Collection of Beatle Oldies

No US release.
UK: Parlophone PCS 7016 — December 10, 1966
No CD release.

- "She Loves You" (**Lennon**-**McCartney**)
- "From Me to You" (**Lennon**-**McCartney**)
- "We Can Work It Out" (**Lennon**-**McCartney**)
- "Help!" (**Lennon**-McCartney)
- "Michelle" (**Lennon**-**McCartney**)
- "Yesterday" (Lennon-**McCartney**)
- "I Feel Fine" (**Lennon**-McCartney)
- "Yellow Submarine" (Lennon-**McCartney**)
- "Can't Buy Me Love" (Lennon-**McCartney**)
- "Bad Boy" (Williams)
- "Day Tripper" (**Lennon**-McCartney)
- "A Hard Day's Night" (**Lennon**-McCartney)
- "Ticket to Ride" (**Lennon**-McCartney)
- "Paperback Writer" (Lennon-**McCartney**)
- "Eleanor Rigby" (Lennon-**McCartney**)
- "I Want to Hold Your Hand" (**Lennon**-**McCartney**)

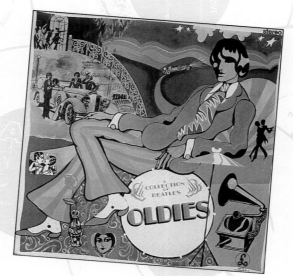

Singles

TITLE	ARTIST	COMMENTS	LABEL/CATALOG NUMBER	RELEASE DATE
A: "Nowhere Man" (**Lennon**-McCartney) B: "What Goes On?" (Lennon-McCartney-Starkey)			US: Capitol 5587 No UK release. No CD release.	February 21, 1966
A: "Paperback Writer" (Lennon-**McCartney**) B: "Rain" (**Lennon**-McCartney)			US: Capitol 5651 UK: Parlophone R 5452 CD: EMI CD3R-5452	May 30, 1966 June 10, 1966
A: "Yellow Submarine" (Lennon-**McCartney**) B: "Eleanor Rigby" (Lennon-**McCartney**)			US: Capitol 5715 UK: Parlophone R 5493 CD: EMI C3-443112	August 8, 1966 August 5, 1966

EPs

TITLE	ARTIST	COMMENTS	LABEL/CATALOG NUMBER	RELEASE DATE
Yesterday ■ "Yesterday" (Lennon-**McCartney**) ■ "Act Naturally" (Russell-Morrison) ■ "You Like Me Too Much" (Harrison) ■ "It's Only Love" (**Lennon**-McCartney)			No US release. UK: Parlophone GEP 8948 No CD release.	March 4, 1966
Nowhere Man ■ "Nowhere Man" (**Lennon**-McCartney) ■ "Drive My Car" (**Lennon-McCartney**) ■ "Michelle" (**Lennon-McCartney**) ■ "You Won't See Me" (Lennon-**McCartney**)			No US release. UK: Parlophone GEP 8952 No CD release.	July 6, 1966

1967

LPs & CDs

TITLE	ARTIST	COMMENTS	LABEL/CATALOG NUMBER	RELEASE DATE

**Sgt. Pepper's Lonely
Hearts Club Band**

US: Capitol SMAS 2653
UK: Parlophone PCS 7027
CD: Parlophone CDP 7 46442 2

June 2, 1967
June 1, 1967

- "Sgt. Pepper's Lonely Hearts Club Band" (Lennon-**McCartney**)
- "With a Little Help From My Friends" (**Lennon-McCartney**)
- "Lucy in the Sky with Diamonds" (**Lennon**-McCartney)
- "Getting Better" (**Lennon-McCartney**)
- "Fixing a Hole" (Lennon-**McCartney**)
- "She's Leaving Home" (Lennon-**McCartney**)
- "Being for the Benefit of Mr. Kite!" (**Lennon**-McCartney)
- "Within You Without You" (Harrison)
- "When I'm Sixty-Four" (Lennon-**McCartney**)
- "Lovely Rita" (Lennon-**McCartney**)
- "Good Morning Good Morning" (**Lennon**-McCartney)
- "Sgt. Pepper's Lonely Hearts Club Band (Reprise)" (Lennon-**McCartney**)
- "A Day in the Life" (**Lennon-McCartney**)

The most elaborate expression of the Beatles' tendency toward innovation, *Sgt. Pepper* firmly established pop music as an artistic medium and the LP as its principal large form. The fact that the album was conceived as an integrated whole forced Capitol to stop putting out slimmed-down U.S. versions of the U.K. LPs. This was the first case in which a Beatle LP was issued in both markets with identical contents.

Magical Mystery Tour

US: Capitol SMAL 2835
UK: Parlophone PCTC 255
CD: Parlophone CDP 7 48062 2

November 27, 1967
November 19, 1976·

- "Magical Mystery Tour" (Lennon-**McCartney**)
- "The Fool on the Hill" (Lennon-**McCartney**)
- "Flying" (Lennon-McCartney-Harrison-Starkey)
- "Blue Jay Way" (Harrison)
- "Your Mother Should Know" (Lennon-**McCartney**)
- "I Am the Walrus" (**Lennon**-McCartney)
- "Hello Goodbye" (Lennon-**McCartney**)
- "Strawberry Fields Forever" (**Lennon**-McCartney)
- "Penny Lane" (Lennon-**McCartney**)
- "Baby, You're a Rich Man" (**Lennon-McCartney**)
- "All You Need Is Love" (**Lennon**-McCartney)

Originally released only in the U.S., the songs on side one were issued in the U.K. as a double EP set.

Singles

Title	Artist	Comments	Label/Catalog Number	Release Date
A: "Penny Lane" (Lennon-**McCartney**) B: "Strawberry Fields Forever" (**Lennon**-McCartney)			US: Capitol 5810 UK: Parlophone R 5570 CD: EMI CD3R 5570	February 13, 1967 February 17, 1967

One of the obvious high points in the Beatles' oeuvre, and widely regarded as the finest single in the history of popular music. According to its original conception, the album that became *Sgt. Pepper's Lonely Hearts Club Band* was to be a reminiscence and distillation of the group's childhood in Liverpool, a theme they had already explored in "In My Life."

Paul's initial efforts resulted in "Penny Lane," a sensuously straightforward evocation of a crossroads near his childhood home. John offered the oddly evasive "Strawberry Fields Forever." The lyric invoked the name of an orphanage near his home as a refuge amidst the confusion and surreality of everyday life. Both productions are among the artists' greatest works.

A number of bootleg issues of "Strawberry Fields Forever" detail the many steps involved in arriving at the final musical arrangement and producing the final recording. John began by strumming the chords on an acoustic guitar, and soon rifled through a catalog of standard picking patterns. The earliest studio version displays a great deal of obvious experimentation in the arrangement, with prominent background vocals and psychedelic guitar effects. The band came back for a second try, and recorded the song as a dreamy rock ballad. Dissatisfied with the results achieved so far, John asked George Martin to score the song for orchestral instruments, and a third, more intense version was recorded.

In the end, John couldn't decide which he preferred—the slower, more serene band rendition, or the faster, orchestrated version. Martin was dumbfounded when John asked him to edit them together, to begin the song with the first approach and end it with the latter. After much protesting, Martin went to work.

To his great surprise, Martin found that by adjusting the playback speed of the two recordings, he could make them match in pitch and tempo. Thus, the final version consists of two entirely different arrangements—conceived, performed, and recorded separately—then spliced together to produce a seamless whole.

| A: "All You Need Is Love" (**Lennon**-McCartney) B: "Baby, You're a Rich Man" (**Lennon-McCartney**) | | | US: Capitol 5964 UK: Parlophone R 5620 CD: EMI C3-44316 | July 17, 1967 July 7, 1967 |

Some of the tracks for side A were recorded live during the worldwide broadcast of *Our World* on June 25, 1967.

Our World was a landmark in television history, the first live intercontinental satellite broadcast, estimated to have reached 400 million viewers in twenty-five countries. The Beatles hosted Britain's contribution to the five-hour program and performed a song written especially for the occasion.

Although the musical performance appeared on television to have been truly live, most of the Beatles' instrumental tracks and background vocals had been recorded over the previous several days. On the day of the broadcast, the Fabs were joined at EMI by a thirteen-member orchestra (conducted by George Martin) and a large group of colorfully dressed friends, including Mick Jagger, Marianne Faithful, Keith Richards, Keith Moon, Mike McGear, Eric Clapton, Jane Asher, and Graham Nash.

On the recording of "All You Need Is Love" is a remix of the broadcast version with a new lead vocal by John.

| A: "Hello Goodbye" (Lennon-**McCartney**) B: "I Am the Walrus" (**Lennon**-McCartney) | | | US: Capitol 2056 UK: Parlophone R 5655 CD: EMI C3-44317 | November 27, 1967 November 24, 1967 |

EPs

TITLE	ARTIST	COMMENTS	LABEL/CATALOG NUMBER	RELEASE DATE

Magical Mystery Tour

No US release.
UK: Parlophone SMMT 1/2   December 8, 1967
No CD release.

- "Magical Mystery Tour" (Lennon-**McCartney**)
- "Your Mother Should Know" (Lennon-**McCartney**)
- "I Am the Walrus" (**Lennon**-McCartney)
- "The Fool on the Hill" (Lennon-**McCartney**)
- "Flying" (Lennon-McCartney-Harrison-Starkey)
- "Blue Jay Way" (Harrison)

A double-EP set containing songs from the made-for-TV film, this package is equivalent to side one of the U.S. LP of the same name. The LP was not made available in the U.K. until 1976.

On the set of the *Our World* broadcast, for which the Beatles performed "All You Need Is Love" live via satellite on June 25, 1967.

1968

LPs & CDs

TITLE	ARTIST	COMMENTS	LABEL/CATALOG NUMBER	RELEASE DATE

The Beatles

(also known as the

White Album)

- "Back in the USSR" (Lennon-**McCartney**)
- "Dear Prudence" (**Lennon**-McCartney)
- "Glass Onion" (**Lennon**-McCartney)
- "Ob-La-Di, Ob-La-Da" (Lennon-**McCartney**)
- "Wild Honey Pie" (Lennon-**McCartney**)
- "The Continuing Story of Bungalow Bill" (**Lennon**-McCartney)
- "While My Guitar Gently Weeps" (Harrison)
- "Happiness Is a Warm Gun" (**Lennon**-McCartney)
- "Martha My Dear" (Lennon-**McCartney**)
- "I'm So Tired" (**Lennon**-McCartney)
- "Blackbird" (Lennon-**McCartney**)
- "Piggies" (Harrison)
- "Rocky Racoon" (Lennon-**McCartney**)
- "Don't Pass Me By" (Starkey)
- "Why Don't We Do It in the Road?" (Lennon-**McCartney**)
- "I Will" (Lennon-**McCartney**)
- "Julia" (**Lennon**-McCartney)
- "Birthday" (Lennon-**McCartney**)
- "Yer Blues" (**Lennon**-McCartney)
- "Mother Nature's Son" (Lennon-**McCartney**)
- "Everybody's Got Something to Hide Except for Me and My Monkey" (**Lennon**-McCartney)
- "Sexy Sadie" (**Lennon**-McCartney)
- "Helter Skelter" (Lennon-**McCartney**)
- "Long, Long, Long" (Harrison)
- "Revolution 1" (**Lennon**-McCartney)
- "Honey Pie" (Lennon-**McCartney**)
- "Savoy Truffle" (Harrison)
- "Cry Baby Cry" (**Lennon**-McCartney)
- "Revolution 9" (**Lennon**-McCartney)
- "Good Night" (**Lennon**-McCartney)

US: Apple SWBO 101
UK: Apple PCS 7067/8
CD: Parlophone CDP 7 46443/4 2

November 25, 1968
November 22, 1968

Much has been made of the fact that many of the songs on the White Album were recorded by one or two Beatles without the others, leading to the proposition that most of the creative work of the group was done by individual members, rather than as a team. On the other hand, most of the songs were written between mid-February and late March 1968 at the Maharishi's retreat in Rishikesh, India, where John, Paul, and George met nightly for long outdoor jam sessions.

It does appear to be true that the White Album sessions sowed the seeds of the Beatles' breakup. Tension rose as John brought Yoko into the studio—the first time Beatle wives had been allowed in—and he even set up a bed for her when she fell ill. Business meetings for the newly formed Apple Corps. interrupted sessions, and guests were allowed to distract the musicians for hours on end. Musical differences, made brutally explicit in John's avant-garde collage "Revolution 9," erupted into arguments, which led Ringo to quit the band between August 22 and September 5, 1968.

The music, however, is among the strongest of the group's career. The songs are masterfully expressive. The dizzying variety of styles is complemented by superb arrangements and performances, conveying a sense of spontaneity that the group had not matched since their earliest records. Even after the dramatic progress of 1967, the Beatles continued to grow.

Ringo with Fab recording engineer Geoff Emerick in 1968. Emerick was awarded a Grammy by America's National Academy of Recording Arts and Sciences for his contribution to *Sgt. Pepper's Lonely Hearts Club Band.*

Singles

TITLE	ARTIST	COMMENTS	LABEL/CATALOG NUMBER	RELEASE DATE
A: "Lady Madonna"			US: Capitol 2138	March 18, 1968
(Lennon-**McCartney**)			UK: Parlophone R 5675	March 15, 1968
B: "The Inner Light"			CD: EMI C3-44318	
(Harrison)				

The only Beatle to appear on the B-side is George. He is accompanied by an Indian ensemble recorded in Bombay during sessions for his *Wonderwall* soundtrack [US: Apple ST-3350 (1968)]. The lyrics are lifted almost directly from the *Tao Te Ching*.

A: "Hey Jude"			US: Apple 2276	August 26, 1968
(Lennon-**McCartney**)			UK: Apple R 5722	August 30, 1968
B: "Revolution"			CD: EMI C3-44319	
(**Lennon**-McCartney)				

The first release on the Beatles' own label, Apple Records.

1969

LPs & CDs

TITLE	ARTIST	COMMENTS	LABEL/CATALOG NUMBER	RELEASE DATE

Yellow Submarine

(soundtrack)

- "Yellow Submarine" (Lennon-**McCartney**)
- "Only a Northern Song" (Harrison)
- "All Together Now" (Lennon-**McCartney**)
- "Hey Bulldog" (**Lennon**-McCartney)
- "It's All Too Much" (Harrison)
- "All You Need Is Love" (**Lennon**-McCartney)
- Plus additional titles composed, arranged, and performed by George Martin & Orchestra.

Some anomalies: "Hey Bulldog" appears only in the U.K. version of the film, and "It's All Too Much" has an extra verse in the actual film soundtrack. From the tone of the performances and the sound of the recordings, it appears that very little care was taken with the four new songs introduced on this album.

US: Apple SW 153
UK: Apple PCS 7070
CD: Parlophone CDP 7 46445 2

January 13, 1969
January 17, 1969

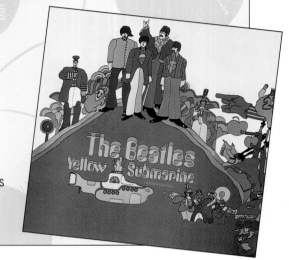

Abbey Road

- "Come Together" (**Lennon**-McCartney)
- "Something" (Harrison)
- "Maxwell's Silver Hammer" (Lennon-**McCartney**)
- "Oh! Darling" (Lennon-**McCartney**)
- "Octopus' Garden" (Starkey)
- "I Want You (She's So Heavy)" (**Lennon**-McCartney)
- "Here Comes the Sun" (Harrison)
- "Because" (**Lennon**-McCartney)
- "You Never Give Me Your Money" (Lennon-**McCartney**)
- "Sun King" (**Lennon**-McCartney)
- "Mean Mr. Mustard" (**Lennon**-McCartney)
- "Polythene Pam" (**Lennon**-McCartney)
- "She Came in Through the Bathroom Window" (Lennon-**McCartney**)
- "Golden Slumbers" (Lennon-**McCartney**)
- "Carry That Weight" (Lennon-**McCartney**)
- "The End" (Lennon-**McCartney**)
- "Her Majesty" (Lennon-**McCartney**)

US: Apple SO 383
UK: Apple PCS 7088
CD: Parlophone CDP 7 46446 2

October 1, 1969
September 26, 1969

The final Beatle album to be recorded, *Abbey Road* was nonetheless released before *Let It Be*. Held up by disagreements over its content, as well as plans to issue a book, an LP, and a film simultaneously, *Let It Be* became the Beatles' final new release.

TITLE	ARTIST	COMMENTS	LABEL/CATALOG NUMBER	RELEASE DATE
No One's Gonna Change various artists **Our World**			No US release. UK: Regal Zonophone Star Line SRS 5013 No CD release.	December 12, 1969

- "Across the Universe" (**Lennon**-McCartney)   World Wildlife Federation version.
- Plus songs by other artists, including the
  Bee Gees, the Hollies, Cliff Richard.

Originally recorded in early February 1968, "Across the Universe" was shelved soon thereafter due to John's dissatisfaction with its production.

When British comedian Spike Milligan asked the Beatles for a donation to a superstar compilation album, proceeds from which were to benefit the World Wildlife Federation, the abandoned song seemed the perfect candidate. The record received limited distribution, so few recognized the song when it reappeared six months later, substantially overdubbed and remixed by Phil Spector, on *Let It Be*.

The original version can be found on the 1988 compilation *Past Masters Volume Two*.

Singles

TITLE	ARTIST	COMMENTS	LABEL/CATALOG NUMBER	RELEASE DATE
A: **"Get Back"** (Lennon-**McCartney**) B: **"Don't Let Me** **Down"** (**Lennon**-McCartney)	The Beatles with Billy Preston	Single take, different from LP.	US: Apple 2490 UK: Apple R 5777 CD: EMI C3-44320	May 5, 1969 April 11, 1969
A: **"The Ballad of John** **and Yoko"** (**Lennon**-McCartney) B: **"Old Brown Shoe"** (Harrison)			US: Apple 2531 UK: Apple R 5786 CD: EMI C3-44313	June 4, 1969 May 30, 1969

George and Ringo didn't participate in the recording of side A. John plays guitar and sings; Paul plays drums, piano, and percussion and sings.

TITLE	ARTIST	COMMENTS	LABEL/CATALOG NUMBER	RELEASE DATE
A: **"Something"** (Harrison) B: **"Come Together"** (**Lennon**-McCartney)			US: Apple 2654 UK: Apple R 5814 CD: EMI C3-44314	October 6, 1969 October 31, 1969

1970

LPs & CDs

TITLE	ARTIST	COMMENTS	LABEL/CATALOG NUMBER	RELEASE DATE

Hey Jude

(also known as *The Beatles Again*)

- "Can't Buy Me Love" (Lennon-**McCartney**)
- "I Should Have Known Better" (**Lennon**-McCartney)
- "Paperback Writer" (Lennon-**McCartney**)
- "Rain" (**Lennon**-McCartney)
- "Lady Madonna" (Lennon-**McCartney**)
- "Revolution" (**Lennon**-McCartney)
- "Hey Jude" (Lennon-**McCartney**)
- "Old Brown Shoe" (Harrison)
- "Don't Let Me Down" (**Lennon**-McCartney)
- "The Ballad of John and Yoko" (**Lennon**-McCartney)

An LP compilation of songs that had previously appeared only on singles in both the U.K. and the U.S. It has since been superceded by *Past Masters Volumes One* and *Two*.

US: Apple SW 385
(also SO 385)
UK: Parlophone PCS 7184
No CD release.

February 26, 1970

May 11, 1979

Let It Be

(soundtrack)

- "Two of Us" (Lennon-**McCartney**)
- "I Dig a Pony" (**Lennon**-McCartney)
- "Across the Universe" (**Lennon**-McCartney)
- "I Me Mine" (Harrison)
- "Dig It" (Lennon-McCartney-Harrison-Starkey)
- "Let It Be" (Lennon-**McCartney**)   LP mix, different from single.
- "Maggie Mae" (trad., arr. Lennon-McCartney-Harrison-Starkey)
- "I've Got a Feeling" (**Lennon-McCartney**)
- "One After 909" (**Lennon**-McCartney)
- "The Long and Winding Road" (Lennon-**McCartney**)
- "For You Blue" (Harrison)
- "Get Back" (Lennon-**McCartney**)   LP take, different from single.

US: Apple AR 34001
UK: Apple PXS 1
CD: Parlophone CDP 7 46447 2

May 18, 1970

May 8, 1970

In its original U.K. issue, *Let It Be* was packaged in a slipcase, along with a book containing photographs and unused dialogue from the movie (*The Beatles Get Back*, edited by Jonathan Cott and David Dalton). Unfortunately, the book raised the price of the record, and sales suffered; it was removed and the box slimmed to a gatefold cover for subsequent release.

(See chapter five, "The Beatles on Film: Feature Films," p. 106.)

(See chapter six, "The Beatles in Print: A Selected Bibliography," p. 116.)

Singles

TITLE	ARTIST	COMMENTS	LABEL/CATALOG NUMBER	RELEASE DATE
A: "Let It Be" (Lennon-**McCartney**) B: "You Know My Name (Look Up the Number)" (**Lennon**-McCartney)		Single version, different from LP.	US: Apple 2764 UK: Apple R 5833 CD: EMI C3-44315	March 11, 1970 March 6, 1970

Far from a new recording, the B-side—one of the more obscure Beatle songs—was actually finished in June 1967. After a few overdubs, it was remixed in April 1969, and sat on the shelf for almost another year before its release.

Curiously, in late 1969 John tried to issue the song, credited to the Plastic Ono Band, as the B-side to an equally off-the-wall White Album outtake called "What's the New Maryjane" (reportedly composed by John with help from "Magic Alex" Mardas). The single was withheld for unknown reasons, and the song remains unreleased.

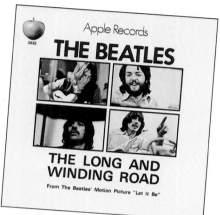

| A: "The Long and Winding Road" (Lennon-**McCartney**) B: "For You Blue" (Harrison) | | | US: Apple 2832 No UK release. No CD release. | May 11, 1970 |

Paul performing on the Apple rooftop during the filming of *Let It Be*.

Post-Breakup Releases and Selected Reissues

LPs & CDs

TITLE	ARTIST	COMMENTS	LABEL/CATALOG NUMBER	RELEASE DATE

Live! At the Star-Club In Hamburg, Germany; 1962

US: Lingasong LS-2-7001
UK: Lingasong LNL 1
CD: Various foreign releases.

June 13, 1977
May 25, 1977

- "I'm Gonna Sit Right Down and Cry (Over You)" (Thomas-Biggs) — US only.
- "Roll Over Beethoven" (Berry)
- "Hippy Hippy Shake" (Romero)
- "Sweet Little Sixteen" (Berry)
- "Lend Me Your Comb" (Twomey-Wise-Weisman)
- "Your Feets Too Big" (Benson-Fisher)
- "Where Have You Been All My Life" (Mann-Weil) — US only.
- "Mr. Moonlight" (Johnson)
- "A Taste of Honey" (Marlow-Scott)
- "Besame Mucho" (Valazquez-Skylar)
- "Till There Was You" (Willson) — US only.
- "Kansas City/Hey Hey Hey Hey!" (Leiber-Stoller/Penniman)
- "Nothin' Shakin' (But the Leaves on the Trees)" (Colacrai-Fontaine-Lampert-Cleveland)
- "To Know Him Is to Love Him" (Spector)
- "Little Queenie" (Berry)
- "Falling in Love Again (Can't Help It)" (Lerner-Hollander)
- "Sheila" (Rowe) — US only.
- "Be-Bop-A-Lula" (Vincent-Davis) — Lead vocal by Star-Club waiter Horst Obber.
- "Hallelujah! I Love Her So" (Charles) — Lead vocal by Star-Club waiter Horst Obber.
- "Red Sails in the Sunset" (Kennedy-Williams)
- "Everybody's Trying to Be My Baby" (Perkins)
- "Matchbox" (trad., arr. Perkins)
- "I'm Talking About You" (Berry)
- "Shimmy Shake" (South-Land)
- "Long Tall Sally" (Johnson-Penniman-Blackwell)
- "I Remember You" (Mercer-Schertzinger)
- "I Saw Her Standing There" (Lennon-**McCartney**) — UK only.
- "Twist and Shout" (Medley-Russell) — UK only.
- "Reminiscing" (Curtis) — UK only.
- "Ask Me Why" (**Lennon**-McCartney) — UK only.

Having played in several Merseyside bands before becoming manager of the Star-Club in Hamburg, Adrian Barber is said to have recorded several Liverpool groups there between December 18 and 31, 1962. A few reels' worth of Beatle shows, generally accepted to have been recorded on January 31, 1962, found their way into the hands of Edward "Kingsize" Taylor, another denizen of the Mersey scene.

In 1964, Taylor tried to sell the tapes to Brian Epstein, who turned them down without realizing that, given the Beatles' recording contract, legally they were the property of EMI. Taylor gave them to a recording engineer who left them behind when he abandoned his offices, where erstwhile Beatle agent Allan Williams found them in 1972. Williams, after being turned down by George and Ringo, managed to sell the tapes to BUK Records, which spent £50,000 improving their rather poor sound quality.

Upon the release of *Live! At The Star-Club*, the Beatles sued BUK and Williams, in hopes of keeping the record off the market. The judge did not find in favor of the Fab Four.

The Star-Club tapes, although of marginal fidelity, do offer a fascinating glimpse of the early Beatles performing before an enthusiastic nightclub crowd. They are sloppy and raucous, with a manic edge befitting of the punk era (which was in full swing by 1977, when the record was released).

Nineteen of the thirty Star-Club songs have not been officially released in any other form, adding quite a large number of songs to the available repertoire. Standouts include "Red Sails in the Sunset," sung by Paul in the manner of the Decca audition's "September in the Rain," and John's rocking "I'm Talking About You."

The downside is the quality of the recording, which leaves much to be desired, £50,000 worth of enhancement notwithstanding. The Beatles performed several of the otherwise unreleased songs for the BBC and/or the Decca audition, which means that better recordings may become widely available sooner or later. Still, many songs appear only in Star-Club performances:

"Your Feets Too Big" (Benson-Fisher)
"Where Have You Been All My Life" (Mann-Weil)
"Little Queenie" (Berry)
"Falling in Love Again (Can't Help It)" (Lerner-Hollander)
"Sheila" (Rowe)
"Be-Bop-A-Lula" (Vincent-Davis)
"Red Sails in the Sunset" (Kennedy-Williams)
"Shimmy Shake" (South-Land)
"I Remember You" (Mercer-Schertzinger)
"Reminiscing" (Curtis)

TITLE	ARTIST	COMMENTS	LABEL/CATALOG NUMBER	RELEASE DATE

The Beatles Live at the Hollywood Bowl

- "Twist and Shout" (Medley-Russell)
- "She's a Woman" (Lennon-**McCartney**)
- "Dizzy Miss Lizzy" (Williams)
- "Ticket to Ride" (**Lennon**-McCartney)
- "Can't Buy Me Love" (Lennon-**McCartney**)
- "Things We Said Today" (Lennon-**McCartney**)
- "Roll Over Beethoven" (Berry)
- "Boys" (Dixon-Farrell)
- "A Hard Day's Night" (**Lennon**-McCartney)
- "Help!" (**Lennon**-McCartney)
- "All My Loving" (Lennon-**McCartney**)
- "She Loves You" (Lennon-**McCartney**)
- "Long Tall Sally" (Johnson-Penniman-Blackwell)

US: Capitol SMAS 11638
UK: EMI EMTV 4
No CD release.

May 4, 1977
May 6, 1977

Finally, a glimpse of the Fabs in concert at the height of Beatlemania. The group's appearances at the Hollywood Bowl on August 23, 1964, and August 30, 1965, were recorded by Capitol for a projected live album. In both cases, when George Martin received the three-track tapes, he found them too crude to work with, and the idea was abandoned.

In 1977, at the request of Capitol's president, Martin took a second listen and decided that perhaps the tapes could be salvaged. In fact, the audio quality of the album is quite acceptable, and fortunately—unlike many live tapes from that era—the recordings capture the Fab Four in excellent form: musically tight, in tune, and surrounded by thousands of screaming fans. Martin's restoration is just about the only hi-fi opportunity to hear just how exciting a Beatles concert could be.

TITLE	ARTIST	COMMENTS	LABEL/CATALOG NUMBER	RELEASE DATE

The Beatles Collection

Includes every UK
Beatle LP except:
A Collection of Beatle Oldies and
Magical Mystery Tour. Includes the
bonus album:

US: Capitol BC 13
UK: Parlophone BC 13
No CD release.

December 1, 1978
November 10, 1978

Rarities

US: Capitol SPRO 8969
UK: Parlophone PSLP 261

- "Across The Universe" (**Lennon**-McCartney) — World Wildlife Federation version.
- "Yes It Is" (**Lennon**-McCartney)
- "This Boy" (**Lennon**-McCartney)
- "The Inner Light" (Harrison)
- "I'll Get You" (**Lennon**-McCartney)
- "Thank You Girl" (**Lennon-McCartney**)
- "Komm, Gib Mir Deine Hand" (**Lennon-McCartney**-Nicolas-Hellmer) — UK only.
- "I Want to Hold Your Hand" (**Lennon-McCartney**) — US only.
- "You Know My Name (Look Up the Number)" (**Lennon**-McCartney)
- "Sie Leibt Dich" (**Lennon-McCartney**-Nicolas-Montague) — UK only.
- "She Loves You" (**Lennon-McCartney**) — US only.
- "Rain" (**Lennon**-McCartney)
- "She's a Woman" (Lennon-**McCartney**)
- "Matchbox" (trad., arr. Perkins)
- "I Call Your Name" (**Lennon**-McCartney)
- "Bad Boy" (Williams)
- "Slow Down" (Williams)
- "I'm Down" (Lennon-**McCartney**)
- "Long Tall Sally" (Johnson-Penniman-Blackwell)

During 1976, EMI reissued each of the Beatles' singles. Two years later, a similar reissue program for LPs took the form of this deluxe boxed set, complete with thirteen albums and a poster. In the U.K., the box constituted a rerelease of nearly every Beatle LP. In the U.S., it represented the initial release of the first seven albums in their fourteen-song U.K. versions, generally acknowledged to have been superior to their U.S. counterparts in both song selection and audio quality.

Despite the addition of the bonus disk *Rarities*, (which fills in gaps created by U.K. singles, but contains little unfamiliar to American ears), *The Beatles Collection* falls short of being a comprehensive set. Over twenty officially released Beatle songs—all from U.K. singles—are missing, including such essential works as "Hey Jude" (Lennon-**McCartney**) and "Strawberry Fields Forever" (**Lennon**-McCartney).

Incidentally, the *Rarities* of the boxed set is not the same LP as that released on March 24, 1980 (only in the U.S.). This *Rarities* was released separately in the U.K. as Parlophone PCM 1001. Both versions, however, have been obviated by the official U.S. release of the U.K. LPs and the two *Past Masters* compilations.

TITLE	ARTIST	COMMENTS	LABEL/CATALOG NUMBER	RELEASE DATE

Rarities

US: Capitol SHAL 12060
No comparable UK release.
No CD release.

March 24, 1980

- "Love Me Do" (**Lennon-McCartney**) — Ringo plays drums, unlike the single version, which features the drumming of session player Andy White.
- "Misery" (**Lennon-McCartney**) — Difficult to find in the US previous to the stateside release of the UK LPs.
- "There's a Place" (**Lennon**-McCartney) — Difficult to find in the US previous to the stateside release of the UK LPs.
- "Sie Leibt Dich" (**Lennon-McCartney**-Nicolas-Montague) — Unavailable in the US previous to the release of *Past Masters Volume One*.
- "And I Love Her" (Lennon-**McCartney**) — Includes four extra bars during the final tag.
- "Help!" (**Lennon**-McCartney) — Single version, featuring a different lead vocal.
- "I'm Only Sleeping" (**Lennon**-McCartney) — UK mix, featuring different bits of backward guitar.
- "I Am the Walrus" (**Lennon**-McCartney) — Includes a few extra bars of music.
- "Penny Lane" (Lennon-**McCartney**) — Includes an extra trumpet line in the final tag.
- "Helter Skelter" (Lennon-**McCartney**) — Mono mix, difficult to find since the demise of mono.
- "Don't Pass Me By" (Starkey) — Mono mix, difficult to find since the demise of mono.
- "The Inner Light" (Harrison) — Difficult to find previous to the release of *Past Masters Volume Two*.
- "Across the Universe" (**Lennon**-McCartney) — Version one, the rare World Wildlife Federation mix.
- "You Know My Name (Look Up the Number)" (**Lennon**-McCartney) — Difficult to find previous to the release of *Past Masters Volume Two*.
- "Sgt. Pepper Inner Groove" (no credit) — Two seconds worth of chattering, unavailable in the US previous to the stateside release of the UK LPs.

A collection of dubious value, even at the time when its contents were uncommon. For one thing, EMI actually created a few of these "rarities" specifically for the album, which seems a bit extreme. Furthermore, as the bootleg archive attests, this material is of little interest compared to what EMI has kept hidden in their vaults.

On the plus side, the cover features the banned "butcher" cover photo originally used for *Yesterday ... And Today*. Ironically, with the standardization of Beatle LPs and CDs to correspond with the original U.K. LPs, "rarities" from the U.K. (such as "I'm Only Sleeping") are now, one decade later, commonplace, while original U.S. releases—including this one—have become genuinely rare.

The Beatles Box

No US release.
UK: Parlophone SM 701-708
No CD release.

November 3, 1980

Available only by mail, this set of eight LPs with deluxe picture sleeves, packed in a wooden crate marked "From Liverpool," straddles the line between the endless parade of reissue compilations that are absent from this listing (*The Beatles 1962–1966* and *1967–1970*, *Rock and Roll*, *Love Songs*, *Ballads*, *Reel Music*, *20 Greatest Hits*, etc.) and the thirteen-LP *The Beatles Collection*. *The Beatles Box* presents 126 of the 212 Beatle songs released by EMI in chronological order, some of them minor alternate mixes in the manner of the U.S. LP *Rarities*.

There are some odd choices; a relatively minor work such as "All Together Now" (Lennon-**McCartney**) is included at the expense of the more essential "I Want You (She's So Heavy)" (Lennon-**McCartney**) or "Long, Long, Long" (Harrison). The brilliant, if sprawling, White Album is generally underrepresented. There's a lot of great music, though, for fans interested in a large-scale compilation, and completists will want such collector's items as "I Feel Fine" (**Lennon**-McCartney) with whispering before the song begins and "All My Loving" (Lennon-**McCartney**) with a high-hat intro.

TITLE	ARTIST	COMMENTS	LABEL/CATALOG NUMBER	RELEASE DATE

**The Beatles Historic
Sessions**
(CD title: *Live at the
Star Club*)

No US release.
UK: Audiofidelity Enterprises AFELD 1018 September 25, 1981
CD: Overseas 38CP-34

The only release of the Hamburg Star-Club performances to collect all thirty tracks in one package.

**The Complete Silver
Beatles**

US: Audio Rarities AFE AR 2452 September 27, 1982
UK: Audiofidelity Enterprises AFELP 1047 September 10, 1982
CD: See **The Decca Sessions 1.1.62**,
and **Raw Energy.**

- "Till There Was You" (Willson)
- "Take Good Care of My Baby" (Perkins-Cantrell-Claunch)
- "Memphis" (Berry)
- "Sure to Fall (in Love with You)" (Perkins)
- "Money (That's What I Want)" (Gordy-Bradford)
- "Three Cool Cats" (Leiber-Stoller)
- "To Know Him Is to Love Him" (Spector)
- "Crying, Waiting, Hoping" (Holly)
- "September in the Rain" (Warren)
- "Besame Mucho" (Valazquez-Skylar)
- "Searchin'" (Leiber-Stoller)
- "The Sheik of Araby" (Smith-Snyder-Wheeler)

On January 1, 1962, John, Paul, George, and Pete Best filed into Decca's West Hampstead studio for a thirty-minute, nerve-wracking audition, and ran through fifteen songs from their club repertoire.

From a distance, the obvious highlights of the set are a trio of Lennon-McCartney originals which remain unreleased:

"Love of the Loved" (Lennon-**McCartney**)   Also recorded by Cilla Black.
"Like Dreamers Do" (Lennon-**McCartney**)   Also recorded by the Applejacks.
"Hello Little Girl" (**Lennon**-McCartney)   Also recorded by the Fourmost.

A number of other songs from the audition appear nowhere else in the Beatle archive, namely George's "Take Good Care of My Baby," "Three Cool Cats," and "The Sheik of Araby," and Paul's gutsy, swinging "September in the Rain" and "Searchin'."

"Till There Was You" and "Money" were released on the first few Beatle albums, which make for interesting comparisons. Several other songs from the audition were performed during the many BBC broadcasts. Live versions of "Till There Was You," "To Know Him Is to Love Him," and "Besame Mucho," recorded exactly a year later, can be found on *Live! At the Star-Club*. "Besame Mucho" also appears in the film soundtrack to *Let It Be*, performed tongue-in-cheek almost precisely eight years later.

Decca apparently had no interest in releasing the Beatles' audition tape, even after they became internationally famous. The recordings weren't released until the early 1980s, when a handful of enterprising companies realized that their copyright was up for grabs. The legality of such products has only recently been confirmed.

Claims to completeness notwithstanding, nearly all Decca audition packages are missing the three Lennon-McCartney originals. They are, however, widely available as bootlegs.

TITLE	ARTIST	COMMENTS	LABEL/CATALOG NUMBER	RELEASE DATE

Only The Beatles . . .

UK only: Parlophone SMMC 151 — June 30, 1986

A very rare cassette-only release. The only thing worthy of note on this officially sanctioned promotional item (for Heineken beer) is a true stereo version of "Yes It Is" (**Lennon**-McCartney). Otherwise, the song has appeared only in mono and mono-reprocessed-for-stereo. Nine tracks from the White Album and earlier fill out the rest of the cassette.

The Decca Sessions
1.1.62

No US release.
UK: Topline TOP 181 — October 19, 1987
CD: Topline CD 523

First CD release of the material found on *The Complete Silver Beatles*.

Raw Energy

CD only: Romance Records SB 18 — 1988
No UK release.

This CD-only release of the Decca audition (minus, as usual, the Lennon-McCartney compositions) is distinguished from other packages of the same material by producer Shmulik Kleinman's efforts to improve the sound of the original recording. *Raw Energy* has less noise, more bass, and a wider stereo field than other releases of the same material.

Still, the results aren't unequivocally better. Some listeners will appreciate the enhancement, while others will regard it as unacceptable tampering with an invaluable historical document. The contents are identical with those of *The Complete Silver Beatles*.

Past Masters Volume
One

US: Capitol C129 90043 — March 7, 1988
UK: Parlophone BPM1 — March 7, 1988
CD: Parlophone CDP 7 90043 2

- "Love Me Do" (**Lennon-McCartney**) — Ringo on drums.
- "From Me to You" (**Lennon-McCartney**)
- "Thank You Girl" (**Lennon-McCartney**)
- "She Loves You" (**Lennon-McCartney**)
- "I'll Get You" (**Lennon-McCartney**)
- "I Want to Hold Your Hand" (**Lennon-McCartney**)
- "This Boy" (**Lennon**-McCartney)
- "Komm, Gib Mir Deine Hand" (**Lennon-McCartney**-Nicolas-Hellmer)
- "Sie Liebt Dich" (**Lennon-McCartney**-Nicolas-Montague)
- "Long Tall Sally" (Johnson-Penniman-Blackwell)
- "I Call Your Name" (**Lennon**-McCartney)
- "Slow Down" (Williams)
- "Matchbox" (trad., arr. Perkins)
- "I Feel Fine" (**Lennon**-McCartney)
- "She's a Woman" (Lennon-**McCartney**)
- "Bad Boy" (Williams)
- "Yes It Is" (**Lennon**-McCartney)
- "I'm Down" (Lennon-**McCartney**)

TITLE	ARTIST	COMMENTS	LABEL/CATALOG NUMBER	RELEASE DATE

Past Masters Volume
Two

US: Capitol C12P 90044 — March 7, 1988
UK: Parlophone BPM2 — March 7, 1988
CD: Parlophone CDP 7 90044 2

- "Day Tripper" (Lennon-**McCartney**)
- "We Can Work It Out" (**Lennon**-**McCartney**)
- "Paperback Writer" (Lennon-**McCartney**)
- "Rain" (**Lennon**-McCartney)
- "Lady Madonna" (Lennon-**McCartney**)
- "The Inner Light" (Harrison)
- "Hey Jude" (Lennon-**McCartney**)
- "Revolution" (**Lennon**-McCartney)
- "Get Back" (Lennon-**McCartney**)
- "Don't Let Me Down" (**Lennon**-McCartney)
- "The Ballad of John and Yoko" (**Lennon**-McCartney)
- "Old Brown Shoe" (Harrison)
- "Across the Universe" (**Lennon**-McCartney) — World Wildlife Federation version.
- "Let It Be" (Lennon-**McCartney**) — Single version, different from LP.
- "You Know My Name (Look Up the Number)" (**Lennon**-McCartney)

During the late 1980s, more or less concurrently with the CD-format issue of the Beatles catalog, Capitol deleted the original U.S. LPs and replaced them with the U.K. configurations. This left a number of recordings from throughout the Fab Four's career, previously available in the U.S. on various LPs, unavailable except as singles. The two volumes of *Past Masters* remedied this situation by collecting all of the non-LP tracks into a comprehensive, compact double-album set.

Thus, formerly obscure tracks such as George's "The Inner Light," the World Wildlife Federation version of "Across the Universe," and the madcap "You Know My Name (Look Up the Number)" take their place beside such Fab classics as "She Loves You," "We Can Work It Out," "Rain," "Hey Jude," "Don't Let Me Down," and the single version of "Let It Be." All of which is not to mention lesser (but no less essential) songs such as "Old Brown Shoe."

Since their contents originated as singles, these long-overdue collections give the impression of "greatest hits" packages without duplicating material from any other Beatles albums. They make wonderful listening.

The infamous Penny Lane.

Singles

TITLE	ARTIST	COMMENTS	LABEL/CATALOG NUMBER	RELEASE DATE
A: The Beatles' Movie Medley Includes excerpts from:			US: Capitol B 5107 UK: Parlophone R 6055 No CD release.	March 15, 1982 May 24, 1982

- "Magical Mystery Tour" (Lennon-**McCartney**)
- "All You Need Is Love" (**Lennon**-McCartney)
- "You've Got to Hide Your Love Away" (**Lennon**-McCartney)
- "I Should Have Known Better" (**Lennon**-McCartney)
- "A Hard Day's Night" (**Lennon**-McCartney)
- "Ticket to Ride" (**Lennon**-McCartney)
- "Get Back" (Lennon-**McCartney**)   LP take.

B: "I'm Happy Just to Dance with You"
(**Lennon**-McCartney)

The A-side is a cut-and-paste job issued in conjunction with *Reel Music*.

TITLE	ARTIST	COMMENTS	LABEL/CATALOG NUMBER	RELEASE DATE
The Beatles Singles Collection			No US release. UK: Parlophone BSC 1 No CD release.	December 6, 1982

Contains all twenty-six U.K. singles in picture sleeves. All but four of the sleeves were newly designed for this release. A seven-inch (17.5-cm) picture disk was included in sets earmarked especially for export to the U.S. It was released separately a short time later:

TITLE	ARTIST	COMMENTS	LABEL/CATALOG NUMBER	RELEASE DATE
A: "Love Me Do" (**Lennon-McCartney**)			No US release. UK: Parlophone RP 4949	Released separately January 10, 1983

B: "P.S. I Love You"
(Lennon-**McCartney**)

EPs

TITLE	ARTIST	COMMENTS	LABEL/CATALOG NUMBER	RELEASE DATE
The Beatles EP Collection			No US release. UK: Parlophone BEP 14 No CD release.	December 7, 1981

Contains all thirteen U.K. EPs, plus an untitled bonus disc [U.K.: Parlophone SGE 1] including:

- "The Inner Light" (Harrison)
- "Baby, You're a Rich Man" (**Lennon-McCartney**)
- "She's a Woman" (Lennon-**McCartney**)
- "This Boy" (**Lennon**-McCartney)

This blue-boxed companion to *The Beatles Collection* fills in another corner of the U.K. catalog with a reissue of every Beatle EP in its original picture sleeve. Except for the double-EP package *Magical Mystery Tour*, all previously released EPs are in mono. The bonus disc contains true stereo (as opposed to "reprocessed-for-stereo") versions of songs otherwise available in mono only in the UK.

The Christmas Records

Beginning in 1963, each Christmas the Beatles made a special six- or seven-minute recording, which was manufactured as a seven-inch (17.5-cm) flexi-disk and distributed by mail to members of their fan club. The Christmas records take a less formal approach than the group's conventional releases, and offer fans a more personal encounter with the Fabs. Although they are widely bootlegged, none has been commercially released.

At first, the Beatles improvised seasonal carols and thank-you's with their usual off-the-cuff humor, based on scripts written by Tony Barrow. In 1966 and 1967 the production grew more elaborate. The Christmas records reached their peak with 1967's *Christmas Time Is Here Again!*, which featured a fully scripted radio play complete with specially composed jingles, sound effects, incidental music, and an involved series of scene changes.

Despite their light-hearted intent, these recordings invariably reflect the state of the group at the time they were recorded. The first message is fresh and full of surprises. In 1964, they sound tired and eager to get it over with, and occasionally their boredom shows through in 1965's production.

For the 1968 and 1969 records, Paul, George, John (with Yoko), and Ringo made separate Christmas messages, which DJ-turned-producer Kenny Everett intercut with odd sounds and current hits. Although a cynical edge is evident in many of the Christmas records, a hint of outright bitterness managed to creep into George and John's penultimate contributions. The final record finds John and Yoko in the full flush of their avant-garde period, excitedly improvising humorous sketches, and Paul, his usual sincere self, singing an off-the-cuff but very catchy Christmas tune.

By 1970, the Fab Four had, for all practical purposes, split up permanently. In lieu of a new Christmas record, Apple compiled the seven previous messages onto a single LP. This was the Beatles' final Yuletide release, and is a prime candidate for general release now that the Beatles' lawsuits with EMI have been settled.

TITLE	ARTIST	COMMENTS	LABEL/CATALOG NUMBER	RELEASE DATE
The Beatles Christmas Record			UK only: Lyntone LYN 492	December 6, 1963

Features several rousing renditions of "Good King Wenceslas" (trad.), individual messages from the boys (scripted, of course), and a closing chorus of "Rudolph the Red-Nosed Ringo" (Marks).

TITLE	ARTIST	COMMENTS	LABEL/CATALOG NUMBER	RELEASE DATE
Another Beatles Christmas Record			UK only: Lyntone LYN 757	December 18, 1964

"Jingle Bells" (trad.), individual messages, and a closing jingle, "Can You Wash Your Father's Shirts?"

TITLE	ARTIST	COMMENTS	LABEL/CATALOG NUMBER	RELEASE DATE
The Beatles' Third Christmas Record			UK only: Lyntone LYN 948	December 17, 1965

"Yesterday" (Lennon-**McCartney**) serves as an a capella, off-key refrain, interspersed with John's "Happy Christmas to Ya List'nas," "Auld Lang Syne" (trad.), the possible copyright infringement of the Four Tops' "It's the Same Old Song" (Holland-Dozier-Holland), and "Christmas Comes But Once a Year" (unknown).

TITLE	ARTIST	COMMENTS	LABEL/CATALOG NUMBER	RELEASE DATE
The Beatles' Fourth Christmas Record Pantomime: Everywhere It's Christmas			UK only: Lyntone LYN 1145	December 16, 1966

A Monty Pythonesque romp though the Beatles' bizarre sense of vaudeville, this features "Everywhere It's Christmas," "Orowanya," and "Please Don't Bring Your Banjo Back" and such dramatic sketches as "Podgy the Bear and Jasper Visit Felpin Mansions."

TITLE	ARTIST	COMMENTS	LABEL/CATALOG NUMBER	RELEASE DATE
Christmas Time Is Here Again!			UK only: Lyntone LYN 1360	December 15, 1967

A rocking little vamp called "Christmas Time Is Here Again" ties together sketches that revolve around an audition for the BBC. Several fictitious groups perform (including the Revellers singing "Plenty of Jam Jars"), and parodies of British radio fare abound. John closes with a poem, "When Christmas Time Is Over."

TITLE	ARTIST	COMMENTS	LABEL/CATALOG NUMBER	RELEASE DATE

The Beatles 1968
Christmas Record

UK only: Lyntone LYN 1743/4 — December 20, 1968

A collage of odd noises, musical bits, and Fab messages, the 1968 record features Paul's song "Happy Christmas, Happy New Year," John's poems "Jock & Yono" and "Once Upon a Pool Table," and an absolutely frightening rendition of "Nowhere Man" (**Lennon**-McCartney) by none other than the ukelele-toting Tiny Tim (of "Tiptoe Through the Tulips" fame).

The Beatles Seventh
Christmas Record

UK: Lyntone LYN 1970/1 — December 19, 1969

This album features an extensive Christmas visit with John and Yoko at their estate, Tittenhurst Park, during which they spread holiday cheer and play vaguely disturbing "What will Santa bring me for Christmas?" games. George appears briefly and Ringo plugs his film appearance in *The Magic Christian*. Paul sings the charming ad-lib, "This Is to Wish You a Merry, Merry Christmas."

The Beatles' Christmas
Album
(UK title: ***From Then***
to You)

US: Apple SBC 100 — December 18, 1970
UK: Apple LYN 2154 — December 18, 1970

A collection of all seven previous Christmas records. Counterfeit copies of this album are fairly common, and sell for $30–$40. An official copy in near-mint condition is worth $100.

Spoken-Word Releases

Most people like Beatle records for the music, but it can be great fun just to hear the boys speak. In the early days of Beatlemania, one way for a record company to tap the seemingly infinite market for Beatle products was to press into vinyl their public-domain comments, most of which were gathered during press conferences. Radio reporters covering the Fabs got into the act by packaging their exclusive interviews.

Meanwhile, record companies with more official connections put together their own talk disks, which purported to tell "the Beatles' story" to fans. Promotional releases, giving DJs access to an illusory Fab interview "live" in their own studios, also proliferated.

As the Beatles passed from fad to history, such productions took on a more documentary tone. Featuring live broadcast coverage of airport arrivals, press conferences, interviews with fans, and other relics of Beatlemania, these recordings are often the best available way to experience firsthand the constant lunacy that surrounded the Beatles. The recordings also capture the wit, grace, and sheer presence—and lack thereof when their patience wore thin—with which the Beatles handled themselves.

The Beatles' stateside record companies, Capitol, United Artists, Vee Jay, and Apple, released a number of spoken-word items, most of them promotional items for distribution to radio stations only. Apple, in Italy only, issued an outrageous interview with Kenny Everett. What follows is a selection of spoken-word highlights from the Beatles' official record companies:

TITLE	ARTIST	COMMENTS	LABEL/CATALOG NUMBER	RELEASE DATE
"Open End Interview with the Beatles"			US: Capitol PRO 2548/9 No UK release. No CD release.	January 1964

Capitol pioneered the "open-end interview" concept specifically for the Beatles. These productions consisted of a recorded interview from which the questions had been deleted, which allowed DJs to converse with the Fabs "live" on the air. This promotional release featured an interview on side A, and highlights from *Meet the Beatles!* on the flip side. Similar promo records were put together for *The Beatles' Second Album* and *Help!*

The Beatles Story			US: Capitol STHO 2222 No UK release. No CD release.	November 23, 1964

Squeaky-clean biography and interviews by DJs John Babcock, Al Wiman, and Roger Christian of KFWB, with a little Beatle music thrown in to keep the kids happy.

Hear the Beatles Tell All			US: Vee Jay PRO 202 UK: Charly CRV 202 No CD release.	September 1964 January 23, 1981

A superior general-release production in the vein of Capitol's *The Beatles Story*. Interviews with all four Beatles by DJ Dave Hull, and with John by Jim Steck.

Una Sensazionale Intervista Die Beatles + Tre Dischi Apple			Italy only: Apple DPR-108 No CD release.	November 1968

Italy's version of the U.K. promotional introduction to Apple, *Our First Four* (a box including the initial singles by the Jackie Lomax, Mary Hopkin, the Black Dyke Mills Band, and, of course, the Beatles).

In addition to singles by Lomax, Hopkin, and the Iveys, the package includes a seven-inch (17.5-cm) single containing Kenny Everett's interview with the zany—and, from the sound of it, quite intoxicated—Beatles. The conversation was conducted during the White Album sessions, on June 5 and 6, 1968, and includes various ad-lib songs such as "Cottonfields" (Ledbetter), "Goodbye Jingle" (improv.), and "Tiny Tim for President (Tiny Tim for Queen)" (improv.).

Cicadelic Records

Cicadelic (5470 Braesvalley #298, Houston TX 77096) offers a valuable eight-volume series that contains various press conferences and radio interviews. Most of the recordings date from the Beatles First American Tour, providing a concise and entertaining aural history of the period. Highlights include the Beatles' tumultuous arrival in Adelaide, Australia, and John's reluctant apology for his "bigger than Jesus" remark. These LPs have no direct U.K. or CD counterparts, although much of the same material can be found on British and CD-format issues on other labels:

TITLE	ARTIST	COMMENTS	LABEL/CATALOG NUMBER	RELEASE DATE
All Our Loving			US: Cicadelic LP 1963	April 1986
First American Tour-era and *Help!*-era interviews by Tidewater, Virginia DJ Gene Loving.				
East Coast Invasion!			US: Cicadelic LP 1964	September 1985
Interviews with John, Paul, George, and Ringo, as well as Brian Epstein, Derek Taylor, and Neil Aspinall, during the First American Tour.				
From Britain . . . With Beat!			US: Cicadelic LP 1967	June 1987
Radio coverage of the Australasian Tour (June–July 1964) and interviews from September 17, 1964, toward the close of the First American Tour.				
Here, There, And Everywhere			US: Cicadelic LP 1968	March 1988
NEMS press officer Derek Taylor interviews the Beatles in the Bahamas, 1965, during the filming of *Help!*				
Movie Mania!			US: Cicadelic LP 1960	November 1986
Behind-the-scenes interviews from the sets of *A Hard Day's Night* and *Help!*				
Not a Second Time			US: Cicadelic LP 1961	February 1987
Press-conference interviews with John from August 25 and September 13, 1964, and with each Beatle on September 4 and September 8, 1964.				
'Round The World!			US: Cicadelic LP 1965	March 1986
Interviews from Britain (December 10, 1963), the First American Tour (August–September 1964), and the Bahamas (on the *Help!* set, February 22, 1965). Also, radio promos for Peter and Gordon and Cilla Black (originally released to radio stations only as US: Capitol PRO 2720).				
Things We Said Today			US: Cicadelic LP 1962	November 1986
Press conferences from Dallas (1964), Seattle (1964), Los Angeles (1965), and Toronto (1965), plus interviews and radio coverage.				
West Coast Invasion!			US: Cicadelic LP 1966	September 1985
Press conferences, interviews, and radio coverage of the western leg of the First American Tour, August 1964.				

Miscellaneous Spoken-Word Records

TITLE	ARTIST	COMMENTS	LABEL/CATALOG NUMBER	RELEASE DATE
The Beatles Talking About . . .			Holland: Magical History Tour 1984 No CD release.	1984

Includes excerpts from a number of more obscure spoken-word releases, including Murray the K's "As It Happened," John's "KYA Peace Talk," Paul's *Ram* promo entitled *Brung to Ewe By Hal Smith*, the interview from *Una Sensazionale Intervista*, and other pieces from various sources. Possibly a bootleg recording.

The Beatles Tapes from the David Wigg Interviews			US: PBR Intern'l 7005/6 UK: Polydor 2683 068 No CD release.	1978 July 30, 1976

Individual interviews with all four Beatles, recorded for broadcast between 1968 and 1973. This includes discussions of the tensions within the band.

The Golden Beatles	The Beatles and others		US: Silhouette 10015 No UK release. CD: Overseas 30CP-56	July 1985

Excerpts from a radio promo ("Music City/KFWBeatles") and the 1968 *Una Sensazionale Intervista* interview. Various Beatle satires are included, the most entertaining of which is a reunion rap that features realistic impersonations and incorporates a number of obscure Fab references.

Interviews with Pete Best			US: Backstage Records BSR-1111 No UK release. No CD release.	1982

An in-depth interview with Pete Best, during which the group's former drummer discusses his dismissal.

I Apologize			US: Sterling Products 8893 6481 No UK release. No CD release.	1966

A record dedicated to John's press conference remarks in the aftermath of his contention, in 1966, that "the Beatles are more popular than Christ."

Talk Downunder			US: PVC/Raven 8911 UK: Goughsound GP 5001 No CD release.	May 1982 May 1982

Interviews from the phenomenally successful Australasian leg of the First World Tour, including a rare chat with Jimmy Nichol, who stood in for Ringo when he had his tonsils removed. The album is designed as a companion to *The Beatles Down Under* by Glenn A. Baker.

Acetates

Acetate disks are legitimate byproducts of the recording process. Manufactured in small quantities, they are often cut from unfinished tapes as demonstrations or tests, and are meant for the ears of technicians, musicians, and executives only. Furthermore, they tend to wear out after just a few spins on a turntable, which makes them extremely rare finds.

During the years before the Beatles had a recording contract, they took every opportunity to have their music put on an acetate disk. Later, whenever they completed a demo recording or a rough mix of a new song, acetates were cut for George Martin, Brian Epstein, and themselves. Since the original recordings weren't considered finished, they were often misplaced or destroyed, which means that such disks are the only remaining source of a number of Beatle demos, alternate mixes, unreleased songs, and the like. Prized as collector's items, they garner extraordinarily high prices at auction houses such as Christie's, Sotheby's, and Phillips and commonly serve as fodder for bootlegs.

It is said that acetates of demonstration performances were made for every known Lennon-McCartney, Harrison, or Starkey composition. A good number less than that, however, can be accounted for today. Although information regarding their origins, contents, and current whereabouts is extremely sketchy, the disks listed below are among those that have found their way to auction and/or bootleg release.

The following list, much of which was gleaned from the pages of *Belmo's Beatleg News* (see chapter six, "The Beatles in Print: A Select Bibliography," p. 117), details a number of acetate disks that have found their way into the hands of collectors.

TITLE	ARTIST	COMMENTS	LABEL/CATALOG NUMBER	RELEASE DATE
A: "That'll Be the Day" (Holly-Allison-Petty)			Label unknown.	mid-1958
B: "In Spite of All Danger" (McCartney-Harrison)				

This acetate is a tantalizing piece of Beatle history. It was made in mid-1958 at the Liverpool studio of Percy Phillips, and recorded in about fifteen minutes by John, Paul, George, John "Duff" Lowe on piano, and Colin Hanton on drums (and possibly Eric Griffiths on guitar).

The A-side, on which John sings the lead, is, of course, the Buddy Holly classic, "That'll Be the Day" (covered in the mid-1970s by Linda Ronstadt). The flip side is shrouded in mystery. "In Spite of All Danger," Paul reveals in Mark Lewisohn's *The Beatles Recording Sessions*, relies heavily for inspiration on a tune made famous by Elvis Presley—but Paul won't name the song. Despite the label credit, Paul claims "In Spite of All Danger" as his own. "I think it was actually written by me," he recalls, "and George played the guitar solo! We were mates, and nobody was into copyrights and publishing."

The recording engineer erased the master tape after cutting only five or six disks, one for each band member. Lowe put his copy—believed to be the only one still in existence—up for auction in 1981. Paul promptly took legal action and obtained an injunction against the sale of the record; he eventually bought it himself in July 1981 for a price reportedly in excess of £10,000. Although it is rumored that Paul has made a few tape copies for friends, nothing has been heard of the recording since, with the exception of a brief excerpt from "That'll Be the Day," aired during a television tribute to Buddy Holly on September 12, 1984. "That was our first record," Paul explains, as he, George, and John harmonize in the background.

A: "Summertime" (Gershwin-Heyward)			Label unknown.	October 1960
B: German-language sales pitch for shoes				

This acetate was recorded during the session in which the Beatles played with Rory Storm and the Hurricanes on October 15, 1960. Then-Hurricane Ringo Starr joined John, Paul, George, and Lu Walters to "Summertime" (Gershwin-Heyward), while members of the Hurricanes performed "Fever" (John) and "September Song" (Anderson-Weill), neither of which have surfaced in any form.

In his book *Shout!*, Philip Norman notes that the B-side of the initial 78 rpm acetate of "Summertime" was a sales pitch for shoes in German. Mark Lewisohn's *The Beatles Live!* further reports that the only known copy is owned by an Australian collector. To date, this acetate has never been issued as a bootleg or legitimate release.

A: "Like Dreamers Do" (Lennon-**McCartney**)			Decca	January 1962
B: "Hello Little Girl" (**Lennon**-McCartney)				

These two songs were never released in performances by the Beatles, but were recorded at the Decca audition on January 1, 1962. The disks were cut by Decca for in-house use. One copy was auctioned at Christie's, London on August 29, 1986 for £2500.

"Like Dreamers Do" (Lennon-**McCartney**)			Dick James Music	1962

Demo recorded by John and Paul for their publisher, sold at auction for £1,000. It has never appeared as a bootleg.

TITLE	ARTIST	COMMENTS	LABEL/CATALOG NUMBER	RELEASE DATE

"Bad to Me"

(**Lennon**-McCartney)

Dick James Music · 1963

A Beatle performance of "Bad to Me" never has been released, and may not ever have been recorded; the song was given to Billy J. Kramer and the Dakotas. This demo, recorded by John and Paul, was broadcast during the *Lost Lennon Tapes* radio series. A copy was auctioned at Sotheby's on December 22, 1981, for £140.

"Do You Want to Know a Secret"

(**Lennon**-McCartney)

Dick James Music · 1963

Demo by John and Paul of the song from the Beatles' first LP, sold at auction for £350. It is a relatively unique rendition, as George sings the lead in the familiar version. This acetate never has appeared as a bootleg.

A: "Some Other Guy"

(Leiber-Stoller-Barrett)

B: "Some Other Guy"

(Leiber-Stoller-Barrett)

Label unknown. · 1963

Reportedly recorded at the Cavern Club, possibly on the same day as the Granada Television film of the same song (August 22, 1962). Brian Epstein manufactured an unknown number of these disks privately, and offered them for sale at NEMS for £2/6. One copy was auctioned at Sotheby's, London, on December 22, 1982, for £1,100. A Beatles recording of this song has never been released on vinyl; however, the band did record a wonderful performance for broadcast by the BBC.

"One and One Is Two"

(Lennon-**McCartney**)

Dick James Music · 1964

A demo by Paul and John. There is no known Beatle performance of this song, which was released by the Strangers with Mike Shannon. A copy was sold at auction for £250.

Paul's Christmas Album

Label unknown. · 1965

According to Castleman and Podrazik's *All Together Now*, Paul recorded a special Christmas greeting for the other three Beatles, singing, clowning, and acting as master of ceremonies. Only four disks were manufactured; the contents have yet to be made public in any form.

"12-Bar Original"

(composer unknown)

EMIdisc · 1965

This meandering blues jam, in the mold of contemporary recordings by Booker T and the MGs, was recorded for the *Rubber Soul* album but was later abandoned. An oddly undistinguished arrangement, it is one of only three instrumentals recorded by the Beatles (the others being "Cry for a Shadow" and "Flying"). An acetate copy was sold at auction for £1,430.

"Yesterday"

(Lennon-**McCartney**)

Dick James Music · 1965

This is a solo demo of one of Paul's greatest songs, auctioned for £520. It has yet to appear as a bootleg.

"Yes It Is"

(**Lennon**-McCartney)

EMIdisc · 1965

This is said to be an alternate take of the song originally released as the B-side of "Ticket to Ride."

TITLE	ARTIST	COMMENTS	LABEL/CATALOG NUMBER	RELEASE DATE

"The Fool on the Hill"
(Lennon-**McCartney**)

EMIdisc — 1967

Paul recorded this demo of the song from *Magical Mystery Tour* alone at the piano. The acetate was sold at auction for £680.

"I Am the Walrus"
(**Lennon**-McCartney)

EMIdisc — 1967

This alternate take of the song from *Magical Mystery Tour*, which lacks a lead vocal, was sold at auction for £250. It is probably the rehearsal version broadcast during the *Lost Lennon Tapes* radio series.

Magical Mystery Tour

EMIdisc — 1967

This set of four acetates is believed to represent an early idea for packaging the film soundtrack. It includes snippets of dialogue as well as "Aerial Instrumental," a working version of "Flying." The set was auctioned for £450.

"Across the Universe"
(**Lennon**-McCartney)

EMIdisc — 1968-1970

John's "Across the Universe" was alternately labored over and shelved a number of times before its release on the World Wildlife Federation benefit LP *No One's Gonna Change Our World*, and later on *Let It Be* in a vastly different arrangement. John expressed his dissatisfaction with both releases. The first was unduly sped up and littered with animal sound effects, and the second weighed down by Phil Spector's lavish orchestration. This acetate seems to contain an interim version free of these defects. It was sold at auction for £500.

"Goodbye"
(Lennon-**McCartney**)

Dick James Music — 1968

Paul gave this song to Mary Hopkin after recording this excellent demo alone on acoustic guitar. He has mentioned it as one of his favorite unreleased "Beatle" tracks, so it may find its way into general release sooner or later. The acetate was sold at Sotheby's on December 22, 1981, for £140.

"Revolution 9"
(**Lennon**-McCartney)

EMIdisc — 1968

This is an unreleased mix of John's sound collage from the White Album, sold at auction for £880. Another acetate containing a different mix went for £500.

"The Long and Winding Road"
(Lennon-**McCartney**)

EMIdisc — 1969

This is Paul's solo demo for the song from *Let It Be*. It was sold at auction for £400, and another acetate containing an alternate Beatles performance of the song went for £260. Neither recording has found its way into circulation, bootleg, or otherwise.

The Beatles with Yoko Ono
(material unknown)

Apple Corps., Ltd. — 1969

This is a mysterious acetate. Possibly, it contains a jam session featuring John, Paul, Ringo, and Yoko recorded during the *Get Back/Let It Be* sessions, and may have been a contender for release under the Plastic Ono Band moniker.

The Beatles on Stage: Major Concert Appearances

Although the Beatles made their biggest impact through their recordings, they started out as a living, breathing, performing rock'n'roll band, and remained one until 1966. At first, they worked the Liverpool club circuit, playing as often as three times a day. Tours of Britain, Europe, the U.S., and eventually Australia and Asia followed. Everywhere they played, the Fab Four were greeted with adulation of an intensity that was never seen before nor has been since.

The dates and venues of many of John, Paul, George, and Ringo's earliest performances are unknown. Beatle scholar Mark Lewisohn tackled the formidable task of ascertaining the performing schedule of the Quarry Men, and later the Beatles, in his impressive book *The Beatles Live.* He was able to document an amazing number of Beatle performances in the clubs of Liverpool and the surrounding area, and pointed out that he must have missed an untold number of others. After all, the early Beatles played regularly at the Liverpool College of Art, performed at private parties, and booked themselves informally at numerous theaters and dance halls, many of which are long gone. As the Fabs became better known, clubs advertised their appearances and Brian Epstein kept detailed records, which made trailing their performances easier.

Even when they were occupied with daily television, radio, press, and/or recording activities, the Beatles continued to play nearly every night, often more than one set. As Paul observed in an interview in Mark Lewisohn's *The Beatles Recording Sessions,* "Those boys worked!"

Paul and George share an onstage vocal (circa 1964). Opposite, top: Hysterical fans, 1964. Opposite, bottom: The band on stage, 1964.

For the First American Tour, Brian Epstein pioneered the now-common practice of presenting the group at sporting arenas. From a tiny stage in the center of the playing field, the Beatles—amplified by only their usual stage gear—would play to tens of thousands of fans at a time. As can be heard in innumerable bootleg recordings, their music was utterly buried beneath the ecstatic screams of the audiences.

Foreign tours stretched the mayhem out over several weeks, and mob scenes of Beatlemania were an inescapable fact of daily life. By 1966,

John, Paul, George, and Ringo had had enough of touring, and they ceased to function as a performing ensemble.

Rather than list every local appearance of the Quarry Men and the Beatles, this chapter includes only highlights. Their performance schedule beginning in 1964, by which time they were touring extensively outside of northern England, is presented in its entirety. Shows that were recorded in any manner are marked by an asterisk (*), often with some indication of where the recording can be found.

I LOVE the "BEATLES"

John during the late fifties. Stuart Sutcliffe stands in the background.

1957

June 9, 1957: Empire Theatre, Liverpool.

The first verifiable public appearance of the Quarry Men: An audition, unsuccessful, before impresario Carroll Levis for the *Discoveries* television show.

July 6, 1957: Garden Fete, St. Peter's Church, Woolton, Liverpool.

Playing the Woolton Fete was quite a coup for John and his band, and represented the first hint of mainstream acceptance of their unpolished talent and outlandish taste. In fact, it was on this day that John's Aunt Mimi saw John for the first time in full Teddy Boy regalia. She was both outraged and touched when John, spotting her in the audience, acknowledged the confrontation by improvising a lyric: "Mimi's coming, oh, oh, Mimi's coming down the path."

According to various, and varying, accounts, the Quarry Men performed the Del Vikings' "Come Go with Me" (Quick), Eddie Cochran's "Twenty Flight Rock" (Cochran-Fairchild), Lonnie Donegan's "The Cumberland Gap" (trad.) and "Railroad Bill" (trad.), "Maggie Mae" (a traditional, rather bawdy, Liverpool song that the Beatles later recorded in 1969), and/or, perhaps for the first time in public, Gene Vincent's "Be-Bop-A-Lula" (Vincent-Davis).

Paul, at the behest of Ivan Vaughn, had come to the Fete to check out the Quarry Men. He was impressed, although his sense of superiority was bolstered by the observation that John sang the wrong words to most of the songs. In fact, John was prone to making them up himself, but was duly appreciative when Paul wrote down for him, from memory, the lyrics to "Twenty Flight Rock" and "Be-Bop-A-Lula." Paul further distinguished himself by tuning a guitar—the Quarry Men had been paying a more experienced musician to do this for them—and launching into either "Tutti Frutti" (Penniman-LaBostrie), or "Long Tall Sally" (Johnson-Penniman-Blackwell), or, both, which demonstrated the stunning Little Richard impersonation that would become a trademark and a common set closer for the Beatles.

A week or two later, one of the Quarry Men, Pete Shotton, passed McCartney on his bicycle. He stopped and mentioned that John wanted him in the band. Paul thought for a moment, accepted the offer, and went on his way. The seed had been planted that would flower into the Beatles.

August 7, 1957: Cavern Club, Liverpool.

This was the Quarry Men's first appearance at what would become recognized as the home of the Beatles and the birthplace of the Merseybeat. At the time, the Cavern was primarily a jazz club. John tested the prohibition against rock'n'roll by allowing the band's repertoire to stray from skiffle toward Elvis Presley and Carl Perkins. The manager passed him a note onstage: "Cut the bloody rock!" By the time the Beatles left Liverpool, they had played the Cavern 292 times.

October 18, 1957: New Clubmoor Hall (Conservative Club), Broadway, Liverpool.

Paul's debut with the Quarry Men, playing guitar. In an attempt to show off his instrumental prowess, he stepped to the front of the stage for the break in Arthur Smith and the Crackerjacks' "Guitar Boogie" (Smith)—and made an utter hash of the solo. It was clear to all concerned that the band needed a better lead guitarist.

1958

December 20, 1958: Wedding reception for Harry Harrison and Irene McCann Harrison, Speke, Liverpool.

George Harrison, a school chum of Paul's, had met the Quarry Men earlier in the year. He followed the group doggedly and had managed to sit in on guitar enough that John finally relented and let him join. This date, the wedding of George's brother, marked George's first official appearance as the band's new lead guitarist.

1959

August 29, 1959: Casbah Coffee Club, West Derby, Liverpool.

The grand opening of the Casbah, a teen club in the basement of drummer Pete Best's house, and the first of many engagements there for the Quarry Men, and later, the Beatles (see Ken Brown, p. 30).

October 11, 18, or 25, 1959: Empire Theatre, Liverpool.

A second attempt at gaining a spot on Carroll Levis' *Discoveries* TV show. John, Paul, and George played "Think It Over" (Holly) and "It's So Easy" (Holly). They made it to the next round of auditions!

October 26, 27, 28, 29, 30, or 31, 1959: Empire Theatre, Liverpool.

The Quarry Men sang their way through round two, and qualified for the semifinals. Only one more audition stood in the way of their fame and fortune.

November 15, 1959: Hippodrome Theatre, Manchester, Lancashire.

On the way to their first public appearance outside of the Mersey area, the trio changed its name to Johnny and the Moondogs. They got their final shot at *Discoveries* early in the evening. The performance went well, but it so happened that the final judging, based on the audience's reaction as each performer stepped onstage, was to take place late that night—after the last train back to Liverpool. The three poverty-stricken musicians didn't have enough money between them for a night's lodging. They returned home, and never knew whether they would have passed or failed the audition.

1960

April 23, 1960: The Fox and Hounds, Caversham, Berkshire.

The first performance by John and Paul as a duo. Billed as the Nerk Twins, they appeared for the second, and final, time the following night.

Johnny Gentle Tour of Scotland

May 20–28, 1960: (seven shows).

When the Silver Beatles—John, Paul, George, Stuart Sutcliffe on bass, and drummer Tommy Moore—failed their audition to back Billy Fury, one of the few Liverpool acts that attracted a national following, Allan Williams booked them with another of his acts, singer Johnny Gentle.

Early July, 1960: New Cabaret Artists, Liverpool.

The Silver Beatles backed Janice the Stripper. Paul recalled: "Janice brought sheets of music for us to play all her arrangements. She gave us a bit of Beethoven and the 'Spanish Fire Dance.' So in the end we said, 'We can't read music, sorry, but instead of 'Spanish Fire Dance' we can play the 'Harry Lime Cha-Cha,' which we've arranged ourselves, and instead of Beethoven you can have 'Moonglow' or 'September Song'—take your pick …and instead of 'The Sabre Dance' we'll give you 'Ramrod.' So that's what she got. She seemed quite satisfied anyway."

First Trip to Hamburg

German club owner Bruno Koschmeider was persuaded by Allan Williams to take a chance with a Merseyside band. He was pleased with the first group Williams had supplied, Derry and the Seniors, and asked for another. When Rory Storm and the Hurricanes had previous commitments, Williams contacted the Silver Beatles. Drummer Pete Best was recruited hastily to round out the band, and their name was shortened to the Beatles.

Derry Wilkie of the Seniors wrote to Williams to warn him that a group as unprofessional as the Beatles would ruin the chances for all of the other Liverpool bands, but it was too late. The group's booking at the Indra Club in Hamburg was firm.

August 17–October 3, 1960: Indra Club, Hamburg (forty-eight nights).

The Indra was the smaller and more recent of Koschmeider's two clubs; introducing live music there was something of an experiment. Unfortu-

nately, it failed. Neighbors and customers began to complain about the new band's volume and repertoire: Consequently, the German entrepreneur decided to move the Beatles to his rock'n'roll club in the heart of Hamburg's red-light district, the Reeperbahn.

October 4–November 30, 1960: Kaiserkeller, Hamburg (fifty-eight nights).

Koschmeider's move was the right one. The Kaiserkeller audience, a drunken melee almost constantly on the verge of an all-out brawl, was ready for a group of unkempt Englishmen in black leather who shouted *"Sieg Heil!"* and jumped up and down on the stage until the floorboards broke. The Beatles were a hit.

Toward the end of their residency at the Kaiserkeller, the Fabs accepted an offer to play at the rival Top Ten Club. Their relationship with Kaiserkeller owner Bruno Koschmeider—and their visit to Hamburg—came to an abrupt end when the police, acting on an anonymous tip that British youth were playing at the Top Ten Club without the proper documentation, hauled the Beatles off to jail. They were promptly deported.

1961

February 21, 1961: Cavern Club, Liverpool (lunchtime), Casbah Coffee Club, Liverpool (evening), Town Hall, Litherland (late night).

Only one of a huge number of double- and triple-venue days for the Beatles in 1961. The band played nearly every day of this year.

Second Trip to Hamburg

March 27–July 2, 1961: Top Ten Club, Hamburg (ninety-eight nights).

Proper working papers in hand, the Beatles returned to Hamburg to play the Top Ten Club. Their fee was double what it had been at Koschmeider's Kaiserkeller. Over the three months, Stu Sutcliffe eased gradually out of the band to pursue his first love, painting. His role as bass guitarist was taken over by Paul. When the Beatles left Hamburg, Stu stayed behind.

November 9, 1961: Cavern Club, Liverpool (lunchtime), Town Hall, Litherland (night).

It was probably on this day that Brian Epstein first descended the Cavern's steps into the club's thick atmosphere of sweat and sound—as he put it in his autobiography, "a cellar full of noise."

1962

Third Trip to Hamburg

April 13–May 31, 1962: Star-Club, Hamburg (forty-eight nights).

Billed by Epstein as a European tour, this was the Beatles' triumphant return to Hamburg. They arrived, however, to the news that Stuart Sutcliffe, their friend and former bass player, had died suddenly of a brain hemorrhage only a few days earlier.

The new Star-Club outstripped the other Hamburg venues in size, pay scale, and underworld glamour. As house band, the Beatles shared the bill with Little Richard, Gene Vincent, and other stars who passed through town. Hamburg had nothing, however, to match the telegram they received one day from Brian Epstein: "Congratulations, boys. EMI requests recording session. Rehearse new material."

August 17, 1962: Majestic Ballroom, Birkenhead, Cheshire (evening), Tower Ballroom, New Brighton (late night).

Pete Best's final performances as a Beatle. Brian had broken the news to Pete two days earlier. John called the Beatles' first choice, Ringo Starr, at Butlin's Holiday Camp in Skegness, where he was performing with Rory Storm and the Hurricanes. Starr quit the Hurricanes within days and returned to Liverpool.

August 18, 1962: Horticultural Society Dance, Hulme Hall, Wirral, Cheshire.

After two hours of rehearsal, Ringo appeared with John, Paul, and George for the first time as an official member of the Beatles. At the Cavern Club the next day, the group faced angry fans who shouted "We want Pete!" George received a black eye in the ensuing scuffle.

October 28, 1962: Empire Theatre, Liverpool.

The Beatles performed as part of a package show of nine NEMS artists, all managed by Brian Epstein. Little Richard topped the bill.

Fourth Trip to Hamburg

November 1–14, 1962: Star-Club, Hamburg (fourteen nights).

The Fabs return to Germany, for the first time with Ringo, for another successful engagement.

December 9, 1962: Cavern Club, Liverpool.

George Martin realized that the ideal situation for a Beatle recording would be a live taping in a club before a crowd of their most ardent fans. He attended a Cavern performance on this date in order to evaluate the possibility of recording there. His conclusion: The acoustics in the stone-lined tunnel posed too great an obstacle to making a high-fidelity recording.

Fifth Trip to Hamburg

December 18–31, 1962: Star-Club, Hamburg (thirteen nights).*

The final trip to Hamburg. With "Love Me Do" climbing the charts and their schedule filling up with TV, radio, and press interviews, the Fabs were reluctant to return to the Star-Club. Their New Year's Eve performance was recorded using amateur equipment and released in 1977 as *Live! At the Star-Club.* This is virtually the only recording available of the Beatles performing before a nightclub audience.

1963

Tour of Scotland

January 3–6, 1963: (four shows).

Helen Shapiro Tour

February 2–March 3, 1963: (fourteen shows).

This tour featured Helen Shapiro, Danny Williams, Kenny Lynch, the Beatles, the Kestrels, the Red Price Orchestra, the Honeys, and MC Dave Allen. The venues were virtually all cinemas and theaters. In 1971, at his most bitter moment, John insisted that "the music was dead before we even went on the theater tour of Britain."

March 7, 1963: *Mersey Beat Showcase,* Elizabethan Ballroom, Nottingham.

The first of several package concerts featuring NEMS acts, this one headlined by the Beatles.

Tommy Roe and Chris Montez Tour

March 9–31, 1963: (twenty-one shows).

This tour included the Beatles, the Viscounts, Debbie Lee, Tony Marsh, and the Terry Young Six. The billing was changed to put the Beatles at the top after the first night.

At London Airport, fans send the Fabs off on what was to be their final tour, in 1966.

April 5, 1963: Private performance for EMI executives, EMI House, London.

April 19, 1963: *Mersey Beat Showcase,* King's Hall, Stoke-on-Trent.

April 21, 1963: *New Musical Express Poll Winners Concert,* Empire Pool, Wembley.

April 24, 1963: *Mersey Beat Showcase,* Majestic Ballroom, Finsbury Park, London.

April 25, 1963: *Mersey Beat Showcase,* Fairfield Hall, Croydon.

U.K. Tour

May 18–June 9, 1963: (twenty-one shows).

The U.K. tour featured Roy Orbison, Gerry and the Pacemakers, David Macbeth, Louis Cordet, Julie Grant, Ian Crawford, the Terry Young Six, and Tony Marsh.

June 14, 1963: *Mersey Beat Showcase,* Tower Ballroom, New Brighton.

June 16, 1963: *Mersey Beat Showcase,* Odeon Cinema, Romford.

July 8–13, 1963: Winter Gardens, Margate.

July 22–27, 1963: Odeon Cinema, Weston-super-Mare.

August 3, 1963: Cavern Club, Liverpool.

The Beatles' final performance at the Cavern. They shared the bill with the Escorts, the Merseybeats, the Roadrunners, the Sapphires, and Johnny Ringo and the Colts.

August 6–7, 9–10, 1963: Springfield Ballroom, St. Saviour, Jersey, Channel Islands.

August 12–17, 1963: Odeon Cinema, Llandudno.

August 19–24, 1963: Gaumont Cinema, Bournemouth.*

Walter Cronkite introduced the Fab Four to U.S. audiences on November 21, 1963, using footage of one of these performances. Jack Paar also broadcast clips on January 3, 1964.

August 26–31, 1963: Odeon Cinema, Southport, Lancashire.*

Footage from the August 27 show appears in the thirty-minute BBC documentary, *The Mersey Sound,* first aired on October 9, 1963.

Fans crowd the doors of the London Palladium, October 13, 1963.

Brief U.K. Tour

September 4–8, 1963: (five shows).

The Beatles toured with Mike Barry and Freddie Starr and the Midnighters.

September 15, 1963: *Great Pop Prom,* Royal Albert Hall, London.

Brief Tour of Scotland

October 5–7, 1963: (three shows).

October 13, 1963: *Sunday Night at the London Palladium,* Palladium, London.*

Perhaps the British equivalent of *The Ed Sullivan Show* in the U.S., this show brought the Beatles into 15 million British homes. The next day, every major newspaper reported riots outside of the Palladium. According to the *Daily Mirror,* "Police fought to hold back 1,000 squealing teenagers" as sixty men in uniform escorted the Fab Four to their limousine after the show.

As reported in Philip Norman's *Shout,* however, official photographer Dezo Hoffman witnessed a quite different scene. Pointing out that published photographs of screaming teenagers had been cropped down to only three or four anxious faces, he describes the Beatles exit: "Eight girls we saw. Less than even eight." With a few swift strokes of the pen, it seems, Beatlemania was born.

Swedish Tour

October 25–29, 1963: (five shows).

As the Beatles returned to England after the tour, hundreds of screaming fans were waiting on the roof of one of London Airport's buildings. Ed Sullivan, passing through en route to the U.S., noted the commotion.

Autumn Tour of the U.K.

November 1–December 13, 1963: (thirty-three shows).

This tour starred the Beatles with Peter Jay and the Jaywalkers, the Brook Brothers, the Vernons Girls, the Rhythm and Blues Quartet, Frank Berry, and the Kestrels.

The tour took a break for:

November 4, 1963: *Royal Command Variety Performance,* **Prince of Wales Theatre, London.***

Guests on the show that night included Marlene Dietrich, Buddy Greene, Flanders and Swann, and others, but the Beatles were obviously what the crowd came to see.

With the Queen, the Prime Minister, and the rest of Britain's aristocracy in attendance, John introduced "Twist and Shout" (Medley-Russell) with the request: "Will people in the cheaper seats clap your hands? All the rest of you—if you'll just rattle your jewelry."

The remark was televised to 26 million British viewers on November 10, 1963, and in one masterful stroke the Beatles rose above pop music's run-of-the-mill; their image became imbued with wit, intelligence, grace, and charm.

The tour continued:

November 20, 1963: ABC Cinema, Ardwick, Manchester, Lancashire.*

Footage from this show appeared in the eight-minute Pathé News newsreel *The Beatles Come to Town* (1963).

The tour took a break for:

December 7, 1963: Northern Area Fan Club Convention, Empire Theatre, Liverpool* (afternoon), Odeon Cinema, Liverpool (evening).

Broadcast live on the BBC (title: *It's The Beatles!*) before an audience of 2,500 members of the Beatles' Northern Area Fan Club.

December 21, 1963: *The Beatles Christmas Show* **(concert portion only), Gaumont Cinema, Bradford, Yorkshire.**

December 22, 1963: *The Beatles Christmas Show* **(concert portion only), Empire Theatre, Liverpool.**

December 24, 26–31, 1963: *The Beatles Christmas Show,* **Astoria Cinema, Finsbury Park, London.**

The Beatles Christmas Shows featured music and skits by a number of NEMS acts, including Tommy Quickly, Cilla Black, the Fourmost, and Billy J. Kramer and the Dakotas, the Barron Knights, plus Australian sensation Rolf "Tie Me Kangaroo Down, Sport" Harris.

1964

January 1–11, 1964: *The Beatles Christmas Show,* **Astoria Cinema, Finsbury Park, London.**

John and George, with Cynthia and Patti, returning from a holiday in Tahiti, May 1964.

January 12, 1964: *Sunday Night at the London Palladium,* **Palladium, London.***

This was broadcast live on BBC television.

First Trip to France

January 16–27, 29–31, February 1–4, 1964: Olympia Theatre, Paris.*

Some of these performances were broadcast on French radio.

First Trip to the U.S.

The Beatles' mob-scene send-off from London was eclipsed by their enthusiastic welcomes at New York's Kennedy Airport and Washington's National Airport—scenes largely engineered by Capitol Records.

February 11, 1964: Coliseum, Washington D.C.*

The Fab Four's first concert appearance in the U.S., filmed by CBS for closed-circuit showings in U.S. movie theaters.

February 12, 1964: Carnegie Hall, New York, New York.

Upon their return to London Airport on February 22, 1964, the Fabs were greeted by over 3,500 fans.

A photo opportunity in Paris, January 1964.

April 26, 1964: *New Musical Express Poll Winners Concert,* **Empire Pool, Wembley, London.***

Broadcast in the U.K. on ABC television, May 10, 1964, as *Big Beat '64.*

April 29, 1964: ABC Cinema, Edinburgh.

April 30, 1964: Odeon Cinema, Glasgow.

May 31, 1964: *Pops Alive!* **NEMS package concert, Prince of Wales Theatre, London.**

First World Tour

June 4, 1964: K. B. Hallen, Copenhagen, Denmark.*

The first show in which the Beatles' lineup was John, Paul, George, and Jimmy Nichol. Ringo had collapsed on the previous day during a photo session and was confined to a hospital bed. With less than twenty-four hours before the Fabs' scheduled departure, Brian Epstein ordered George Martin to find a replacement. Martin called Nichol, with whom he had worked recently on a session for Georgie Fame. Once the remaining three Beatles—particularly George, who was obstinate—had been convinced that hiring a stand-in for Ringo was the right thing to do, rehearsals were wedged into every available moment before the Copenhagen show.

June 6, 1964: Veilinghal, Blokker, Netherlands.*

Also on the bill for this show were Wanda, Don Mercedes and His Improvers, Ciska Peters, Jack and Bill, the Toreros, Herman van Keekan, the Fancy Five, and Karin Kent. A recording of the show has appeared as a bootleg.

June 9, 1964: Princess Theatre, Kowloon, Hong Kong.

June 12–13, 1964: Centennial Hall, Adelaide, Australia.*

The Beatles' reception in Adelaide, for which thirty thousand fans (in a state with a population of 1 million) mobbed the local town hall, was unparalleled at any time in their career. A recording of the show has surfaced as a bootleg.

BEATLES FIRST U.S. VISIT

1964 ORIGINAL ISSUE COMMEMORATIVE MEDAL

A press conference marking the Beatles' arrival in America, February 7, 1964.

June 15–17, 1964: Festival Hall, Melbourne, Australia.*

Ringo returned to his drum set on June 15, 1964, to an ecstatic welcome. The June 16 show was broadcast in Australia on July 1, 1964, as *The Beatles Sing for Shell.*

June 18–20, 1964: Sydney Stadium, Sydney, Australia.

June 22–23, 1964: Town Hall, Wellington, New Zealand.

June 24–25, 1964: Town Hall, Auckland, New Zealand.

June 26, 1964: Town Hall, Dunedin, New Zealand.

June 27, 1964: Majestic Theatre, Christchurch, New Zealand.

June 29–30, 1964: Festival Hall, Brisbane, Australia.

July 12, 1964: Hippodrome Theatre, Brighton.

July 23 1964: *Night of a Hundred Stars* **charity revue, Palladium, London.**

July 26, 1964: Opera House, Blackpool.

July 28–29, 1964: Johanneshovs Isstadion, Stockholm, Sweden.

August 2, 1964: Gaumont Cinema, Bournemouth.

August 9, 1964: Futurist Theatre, Scarborough.

August 16, 1964: Opera House, Blackpool.

First American Tour

On this tour, the Beatles performed with Jackie De Shannon, the Righteous Brothers, the Bill Black Combo, and the Exciters.

August 19, 1964: Cow Palace, San Francisco, California.

August 20, 1964: Convention Center, Las Vegas, Nevada.

August 21, 1964: Coliseum, Seattle, Washington.

August 22, 1964: Empire Stadium, Vancouver, Canada.*

A recording of the show has appeared as a bootleg.

Ringo gets the spotlight during the Fabs' first U.S. tour.

August 23, 1964: Hollywood Bowl, Los Angeles, California.*

Portions of this performance can be found on *The Beatles Live at the Hollywood Bowl*.

August 26, 1964: Red Rocks Amphitheater, Denver, Colorado.

August 27, 1964: Cincinnati Gardens, Cincinnati, Ohio.

August 28–29, 1964: Forest Hills Tennis Stadium, New York, New York.

August 30, 1964: Convention Hall, Atlantic City, New Jersey.

September 2, 1964: Convention Hall, Philadelphia, Pennsylvania.*

A recording of the show exists in bootleg form.

September 3, 1964: Indiana State Fair Coliseum, Indianapolis, Indiana.

September 4, 1964: Arena, Milwaukee, Wisconsin.

September 5, 1964: International Amphitheater, Chicago, Illinois.

September 6, 1964: Olympic Stadium, Detroit, Michigan.

September 7, 1964: Maple Leaf Gardens, Toronto, Ontario, Canada.

September 8, 1964: Forum, Montreal, Canada.

September 11, 1964: Gator Bowl, Jacksonville, Florida.

September 12, 1964: Boston Garden, Boston, Massachusetts.

September 13, 1964: Civic Center, Baltimore, Maryland.

September 14, 1964: Civic Arena, Pittsburgh, Pennsylvania.

September 15, 1964: Public Auditorium, Cleveland, Ohio.

September 16, 1964: City Park Stadium, New Orleans, Louisiana.

September 17, 1964: Municipal Stadium, Kansas City, Kansas.

When the tour was announced without a Kansas City show, Charles O'Finley, owner of the local baseball team and stadium, promised his community that the Beatles would play for them. To increase the likelihood that this would happen, he offered a fee of $150,000, a world record for a rock concert at the time. Brian Epstein accepted, and the Kansas City show was added to the tour schedule.

September 18, 1964: Memorial Auditorium, Dallas, Texas.

September 20, 1964: Benefit performance, Paramount Theater, New York, New York.

1964 U.K. Tour

The 1964 U.K. tour featured Mary Wells, Tommy Quickly, the Remo Four, Michael Haslam, The Rusticks, the instrumental group Sounds Incorporated, and MC Bob Bain.

October 9, 1964: Gaumont Cinema, Bradford, Yorkshire.

October 10, 1964: De Montfort Hall, Leicester.

October 11, 1964: Odeon Cinema, Birmingham, Warwickshire.

October 13, 1964: ABC Cinema, Wigan.

October 14, 1964: ABC Cinema, Ardwick, Manchester, Lancashire.

October 15, 1964: Globe Cinema, Stockton-on-Tees.

October 16, 1964: ABC Cinema, Hull.

October 19, 1964: ABC Cinema, Edinburgh.

October 20, 1964: Caird Hall, Dundee.

October 21, 1964: Odeon Cinema, Glasgow.

October 22, 1964: Odeon Cinema, Leeds.

October 23, 1964: Gaumont State Cinema, Kilburn.

October 24, 1964: Granada Cinema, Walthamstow.

October 25, 1964: Hippodrome Theater, Brighton.

October 28, 1964: ABC Cinema, Exeter.

October 29, 1964: ABC Cinema, Plymouth.

October 30, 1964: Gaumont Cinema, Bournemouth.

October 31, 1964: Gaumont Cinema, Ipswich.

November 1, 1964: Astoria Cinema, Finsbury Park, London.

November 2, 1964: King's Hall, Belfast.

November 4, 1964: Ritz Cinema, Luton.

November 5, 1964: Odeon Cinema, Nottingham.

November 6, 1964: Gaumont Cinema, Southampton.

November 7, 1964: Capitol Cinema, Cardiff.

November 8, 1964: Empire Theatre, Liverpool.

November 9, 1964: City Hall, Sheffield, Yorkshire.

November 10, 1964: Colston Hall, Bristol.

December 24, 26–31, 1964: *Another Beatles Christmas Show,* Odeon Cinema, Hammersmith, London.

Music and skits featuring the Yardbirds, Jimmy Savile, Ray Fell, the Mike Cotton Sound, Freddie and the Dreamers, Sounds Incorporated, Elkie Brooks, and Michael Haslam.

1965

January 1–16, 1965: *Another Beatles Christmas Show,* Odeon Cinema, Hammersmith, London.

John (circa 1965).

February 18, 1965: Private party during the shooting of *Help!,* Obertauern, Austria.

April 11, 1965: *New Musical Express Poll Winners Concert,* Empire Pool, Wembley.*

Aired in Britain by ABC television on April 18, 1965, as *Big Beat '65.*

First European Tour

June 20, 1965: Palais des Sports, Paris.*

Broadcast on French TV and radio.

June 22, 1965: Palais d'Hiver, Lyons.

June 23, 1965: Velodromo Vigorelli, Milan.

June 25, 1965: Palazzo dello Sport, Genoa.

June 27–28, 1965: Teatro Adriano, Rome.*

A recording of this show has surfaced as a bootleg.

June 30, 1965: Palais des Expositions, Nice.

July 2, 1965: Plaza de Toros de Madrid, Madrid.

July 3, 1965: Plaza de Toros Monumenal, Barcelona.

Second American Tour

These bands toured with the Beatles: the King Curtis Band, Cannibal and the Headhunters, Brenda Holloway, and Sounds Incorporated.

August 15, 1965: Shea Stadium, New York, New York.*

With 55,600 in attendance, this was, at the time, the largest crowd ever assembled for a concert in the U.S. The show was filmed for a TV documentary, which was first broadcast on March 1, 1966.

August 17, 1965: Maple Leaf Gardens, Toronto, Ontario.

August 18, 1965: Atlanta Stadium, Atlanta, Georgia.

August 19, 1965: Sam Houston Coliseum, Houston, Texas.*

Recordings of both the afternoon and evening shows performed on this date have surfaced in bootleg form.

August 20, 1965: White Sox Park, Chicago, Illinois.

August 21, 1965: Twin Cities Metropolitan Stadium, Minneapolis, Minnesota.*

A partial recording of this show has appeared in bootleg form.

August 22, 1965: Memorial Coliseum, Portland, Oregon.

August 28, 1965: Balboa Stadium, San Diego, California.

August 29–30, 1965: Hollywood Bowl, Los Angeles, California.*

Portions of these shows appear on *The Beatles Live at the Hollywood Bowl.*

August 1965: Cow Palace, San Francisco, California.

1965 U.K. Tour

Along with the Beatles, this tour featured the Moody Blues, the Koobas, Beryl Marsden, Steve Aldo, and the Paramounts (an early line-up of Procol Harum).

December 3, 1965: Odeon Cinema, Glasgow.

December 4, 1965: City Hall, Newcastle-upon-Tyne.

December 5, 1965: Empire Theatre, Liverpool.

December 7, 1965: ABC Cinema, Ardwick, Manchester, Lancashire.

December 8, 1965: Gaumont Cinema, Sheffield.

December 9, 1965: Odeon Cinema, Birmingham.

December 10, 1965: Odeon Cinema, Hammersmith, London.

December 11, 1965: Astoria Cinema, Finsbury Park, London.

December 12, 1965: Capitol Cinema, Cardiff.

1966

May 1, 1966: *New Musical Express Poll Winners Concert*, Empire Pool, Wembley.

This fifteen-minute set was the Beatles' final concert in the U.K. It was not broadcast.

Japanese Beatlemaniacs await the group's arrival at Budokan Hall in Tokyo, July 1966.

Brief Tour of Germany and the Far East

June 24, 1966: Circus-Krone-Bau, Munich.*

A recording of this concert exists in bootleg form.

June 25, 1966: Grugahalle, Essen.

June 26, 1966: Ernst Merck Halle, Hamburg.

The Beatles' first return to Hamburg since their rise to fame.

June 30–July 2, 1966: Tokyo, Nippon Budokan Hall, Tokyo.*

Upon their arrival in Tokyo, the Beatles were informed that a militant Japanese student organization considered the use of Budokan Hall for a rock concert to be a sacrilege against the dead war heroes to whom it was dedicated, and had vowed not to allow the Fab Four to leave the country alive.

The Beatles were driven in their limousine through the city's streets, lined with thousands of fans, to their hotel, where they were confined by order of the police. They were allowed out only to perform, before an audience studded with army sharpshooters, and then hustled back to their sanctuary.

Happily, the band escaped the country without incident. It was the first of a series of events that would crystallize the Beatles' decision to stop touring permanently after their upcoming American Tour.

A number of the Tokyo shows are available as unauthorized video productions. They are among the most disappointing examples of the Beatles in concert.

July 4, 1966: Rizal Memorial Football Stadium, Manila.

The Fabs arrived in Manila to one of their warmest welcomes ever, but shortly after leaving the airport, their luggage was confiscated and they were driven under armed guard to a pier, escorted onto a boat, and taken out to sea for about an hour. Then they were returned to their hotel, and were not told why they had been treated this way.

According to Peter Brown's account in *The Love You Make*, the following morning Brian Epstein was awakened by military police who demanded that the Beatles accompany them to a party at the home of First Lady Imelda Marcos. Epstein refused. He insisted that this was the first he had heard of it, that the Beatles were exhausted and needed to rest. Later, watching the news, Epstein saw a report that declared that the Beatles had snubbed the president's wife.

After the concerts, the Fab Four and their entourage were denied all services, from hotel food to taxi cabs. Loading their equipment without any help, the band drove unescorted to the airport, which was swarming with armed guards. Epstein managed to get the plane to wait on the runway as John, Paul, George, Ringo, Tony Barrow, Neil Aspinall, and Mal Evans carted their luggage and equipment through a throng of angry Filipinos. The entourage was kicked, spat upon, and poked with clubs by uniformed men as the mob jeered; punches were thrown as Mal Evans was jumped by six officers.

Finally aboard the plane, there were several delays before Epstein could negotiate their escape. In the process, he gave up the Beatles' cash earnings for the concert.

Third American Tour

The Ronettes and the Cyrkle accompanied the Beatles on this tour.

The third American tour was the last straw for the Beatles as a touring band. An interview, published in Britain without incident five months earlier, was picked up by a U.S. teen magazine called *Datebook*. In it, John was quoted quite accurately: "Christianity will go. It will vanish and shrink . . . we're more popular than Jesus now. I don't know which will go first—rock'n'roll or Christianity."

The furor in America, particularly in the South, was dramatic: Radio stations banned Beatle music, churches sponsored record burnings, record stores stopped reordering, and newspapers went out of their way to condemn John, Paul, George, and Ringo as individuals. At press conferences, John was inundated with demands for an apology; when he tried to explain he simply was shouted down. (The government of South Africa even went so far as to ban the broadcast of Beatle records in response to John's comments; his solo records are banned there to this day.)

The Beatles were also physically threatened, most notably by the Grand Dragon of the Ku Klux Klan. When a firecracker exploded onstage during the Memphis concert, each Beatle looked around to see who had been shot. It was clearly time for the madness to end.

For some time thereafter, John seemed to take pleasure in rubbing salt in the wounds, proclaiming "They're gonna crucify me" in "The Ballad of John and Yoko." Years later, however, he expressed gratitude for some of the more thoughtful reactions he received. "Lots of people sent me books about Jesus," he relates in Hunter Davies' biography, *The Beatles.* "I read a lot of them and found out things . . . I don't know. All I know is that I am being made more aware by it all. I just want to be told more."

August 12, 1966: International Amphitheater, Chicago, Illinois.

August 13, 1966: Olympic Stadium, Detroit, Michigan.

August 14, 1966: Cleveland Stadium, Cleveland, Ohio.

August 15, 1966: DC Stadium, Washington, D.C.

August 16, 1966: Philadelphia Stadium, Philadelphia, Pennsylvania.

August 17, 1966: Maple Leaf Gardens, Toronto, Ontario, Canada.

August 18, 1966: Suffolk Downs Racetrack, Boston, Massachusetts.

August 19, 1966: Mid-South Coliseum, Memphis, Tennessee.

The final public performance of the Fab Four, on the rooftop of the Apple offices, January 30, 1969.

August 21, 1966: Crosley Field, Cincinnati, Ohio (afternoon), Busch Stadium, St. Louis, Missouri (evening).

August 23, 1966: Shea Stadium, New York, New York.

August 25, 1966: Seattle Coliseum, Seattle, Washington.

August 28, 1966: Dodger Stadium, Los Angeles, California.

August 29, 1966: Candlestick Park, San Francisco, California.*

Although it wasn't announced at the time, the Beatles' inner circle knew that this would be the final Beatle concert. Recordings of this show that have surfaced as bootlegs are said to have origi-

nated from a cassette made by Tony Barrow at Paul's request. Rumor has it that the entire show was professionally taped and filmed; no such film or recording has surfaced.

1969

January 30, 1969: Apple rooftop, Savile Row, London.*

Many regard this as the Beatles' last public performance. It was, in fact, the dying gasp of both Paul's plans for a Fab Four comeback tour and for the group itself. Most of the show, performed with spirit for the pigeons and whoever was curious enough to climb to the roof of a neighboring building to find out what the racket was, appears in the film *Let It Be.* The music ground to a halt after nine songs as policemen, responding to complaints from local businesses, pulled the plug.

The Beatles on Film

At the height of Beatlemania, the Fab Four's appeal was as much visual as musical. Like Elvis Presley, they regarded feature films as a logical next step in their careers. Unlike Elvis Presley, however, they were determined that their movies be well scripted, rather than flimsy excuses for face shots and song-and-dance numbers. In this light, *A Hard Day's Night,* an exaggerated documentary, was an unqualified success. *Help!* was somewhat less so, as it placed the stars at the center of a numbing kaleidescope of exotic imagery and absurd situations.

While Beatlemania was still thriving, the Fabs appeared on numerous television shows to perform their music. Most of these were lip-synched, but on rare occasions the Beatles gave live performances, which were filmed in concert halls before an unrehearsed audience—these were the first Beatle concert films. There were also two official attempts to document a Beatle concert: CBS's film of the 1964 Washington, D.C., performance and NEMS's own *Live at Shea Stadium.*

As their artistic aims became more ambitious, the Beatles found it difficult to reconcile their increasingly idiosyncratic powers of expression with the more formulaic demands of pop stardom. They were unable to agree on the script for a third musical comedy feature. Paul's 1967 adventure in film production, *Magical Mystery Tour,* demonstrated that the artists were, at the time, overextended and underinspired. Perhaps in reaction to the *Magical Mystery Tour* experience, they relinquished control entirely to a team of animators interested in creating a fantasy loosely based on their songs in *Yellow Submarine.*

Although it was originally conceived as a grandiose multimedia overstatement, *Let It Be* was perhaps the most appropriate Beatle movie: a humble documentary about the inner workings of a rock'n'roll band. Unfortunately, by the time the film was released, the Beatles had gone their separate ways.

Feature Films

A Hard Day's Night

A Hard Day's Night (1964) is a musical comedy, directed by Richard Lester, American director of the 1959 British hit *The Running, Jumping, and Standing Still Film,* and produced by Walter Shenson, American producer of British hit *The Mouse That Roared,* with Denis O'Dell, later director of Apple Films. The screenplay is written by Alun Owen, Liverpudlian screenwriter known for his vivid renderings of Liverpool slang.

The film stars John, Paul, George, and Ringo, and co-stars Wilfrid Bramble, the only established actor involved, star of the U.K. television sitcom *Steptoe and Son.* Supporting actors include Victor Spinetti as an agitated TV director, Norman Rossington as Norm the roadie (based on Neil Aspinall), John Junkin as roadie Shake (based on Mal Evans), and Kenneth Haigh, who insisted that his name be omitted from the credits. Distributed by United Artists. 87 minutes.

The Fab Four's first film, a low-budget affair costing only $500,000, depicts Beatlemania in full flower. Alun Owen spent several days on tour with the group, and derived several scenes from actual events. The Beatles are chased everywhere they go, meet all authority figures with their irreverent brand of humor, and, for the high point, perform before a crowd of screaming female fans.

The music, a batch of new songs composed specifically for the film, was among the group's best to date: the title song (the first John had ever written on assignment), "Tell Me Why," "And I Love Her," "I'm Happy Just to Dance With You," "Can't Buy Me Love," "I Should Have Known Better," and "If I Fell."

Love interest was left out of the script intentionally, in order to avoid upsetting female fans. In real life, George met his future wife, actress Patti Boyd, on the set.

An incidental flub by Ringo provided the movie's title. Emerging from Abbey Road Studios after a particularly long recording session, he commented "It's been a hard day." Then, noticing the darkened sky, the drummer added "'s night!" John appropriated the phrase for the story "Sad Michael," which appeared in his first book, *In His Own Write.*

John later lamented the imposition of Alun Owen's script on the group's spontaneity, as well as the stereotypical treatment of their individual personalities. But ultimately he was more positive about *A Hard Day's Night* than any of the group's later films. "It was a good projection of one facade of us, which was on tour," he concluded.

Above: Paul and Ringo take a break during the filming of *Help!* Opposite, top: At Twickenham Film Studios, March 1964. Opposite, bottom: The Fab Four (circa 1964).

On Salisbury Plain for the filming of *Help!*

The Beatles Live at the Washington Coliseum

The Beatles Live at the Washington Coliseum (February 11, 1964) is a concert performance filmed by CBS, documenting the Beatles' first appearance in the U.S. The film debuted in U.S. movie theaters March 14–15, 1964 and was telecast (probably in the U.K.) on November 2, 1964. In the film, the Fab Four perform: "Roll Over Beethoven" (Berry), "From Me To You," "I Saw Her Standing There," "This Boy," "All My Loving," "I Wanna Be Your Man," "Twist and Shout" (Medley-Russell).

Help!

Help! (1965) is a musical comedy directed by Richard Lester and produced by Walter Shenson. The screenplay is by Marc Behm and Charles Wood, based on a story by Behm.

John, Paul, George, and Ringo are joined by popular British character actor Leo McKern as High Priest Clang, Eleanor Bron as Priestess Ahme, and Victor Spinetti, retained from *A Hard Day's Night.* Other supporting actors include Roy Kinnear, Warren Mitchell, Peter Copley, and Dandy Nichols. Distributed by United Artists. 90 minutes.

This second Beatle feature takes the zaniness of the first to cartoonish extremes. Off-the-wall fantasy replaces the documentary style of *A Hard Day's Night* in this story of a religious cult's efforts to recover a sacred ring that has become attached to Ringo's finger. The deadpan drummer suffers numerous indignities, including attempted ampu-

tation of the hand and sacrifice to the goddess Kaili, before the affair is over.

Although the Fabs' charm is often buried beneath a labyrinthine plot and heavy-handed production, the music is as bouyant, tuneful, and expressive as ever. Seven new songs were composed for the film: John's title song, "Another Girl," "Ticket to Ride," "The Night Before," "You've Got to Hide Your Love Away," "I Need You," and "You're Gonna Lose That Girl."

Much of the $1.5 million film is occupied with a mad dash between exotic locales: Paul has mentioned that the shooting locations, which included the Bahamas and the Austrian Alps, were selected more for their value as vacation spots than to fulfill requirements of the script.

The film went through a number of working titles before Lester settled on the title of one of John's new songs. Ringo's suggestion, *Eight Arms to Hold You,* actually appeared on the label of the first batch of *Help!* singles.

The critics were less enthralled with *Help!* than they had been with *A Hard Day's Night.* Nonetheless, *Help!* won first prize at the 1965 International Film Festival in Rio de Janeiro. The Beatles themselves were less satisfied, particularly John, who dismissed the film as "crap." Their lack of enthusiasm may explain the difficulty faced by the group in selecting a script for their next feature.

The Beatles at Shea Stadium

The Beatles at Shea Stadium (1966) was produced by Ed Sullivan Productions, Inc. in association with NEMS Enterprises, Ltd. and Subafilms, Ltd. It was originally aired by the BBC on March 1, 1966.

This is the only official concert film produced by the Beatles. It covered their August 15, 1965 performance at Shea Stadium, New York, before the largest concert audience ever assembled in the U.S. The fifty-minute film includes behind-the-scenes glimpses of the preparations, and features brief appearances—complete with go-go dancers—by King Curtis, Cannibal and the Headhunters, Brenda Holloway, and Sounds Incorporated. The Fabs perform: "I'm Down," "Twist and Shout" (Medley-Russell), "I Feel Fine," "Dizzy Miss Lizzy" (Williams), "Ticket to Ride," "Act Naturally" (Russell-Morrison)—with sound dubbed from the studio recording—"Can't Buy Me Love," "Baby's in Black," and "A Hard Day's Night."

Magical Mystery Tour

Magical Mystery Tour (1967) is a fantasy directed by the Beatles and produced by Denis O'Dell for Apple Films. It was originally aired by the BBC on December 26, 1967. 50 minutes.

On an airplane flight between the U.S. and Britain in early 1967, Paul sketched out the basic ideas for the Beatles' first self-penned, -directed, and -produced film vehicle. His idea was that the group would rent a film crew and a tour bus, fill it with people, tour the countryside, and film whatever might happen. The results would be aired on television and provide an hour's worth of escapist entertainment.

Accordingly, the band collected forty-three actors, circus performers, friends, and associates and took to the road. Unfortunately, that's very nearly the whole story. The first project undertaken after Brian Epstein's untimely death, *Magical Mystery Tour* was sorely in need of his vision and organizational skills, which the Beatles had taken for granted for years. No one prepared accommodations for the passengers and crew, and nobody

A scene from the Beatles' second feature film, *Help!*

knew what to do about the hordes of fans that kept traffic gridlocked for miles behind and in front of the bus. A script had never been developed, and very little of interest happened spontaneously.

Despite Paul's six-month effort to edit the footage into a narrative involving a Mystery Tour secretly guided by four ("or five") mysterious magicians, he had very little to work with. John's sequence, in which the obese Aunt Jessie dreams of mountains of spaghetti, is, at least, vaguely unsettling. Even the six songs flounder in their lack of purpose, except perhaps the surreal, if overly cute, treatment of "I Am the Walrus." Five other compositions debut in the film: Paul's title song, "The Fool on the Hill," "Blue Jay Way," "Flying," and "Your Mother Should Know."

None of the film's shortcomings escaped the critics when the show was aired, and *Magical Mystery Tour* became the Beatles' first unqualified flop. This was a rude awakening after the heady breakthrough of *Sgt. Peppers Lonely Heart's Club Band.* Although Paul continues to defend the film as a piece of experimental television, viewed from a vantage point of nearly twenty-five years, it is still remarkably directionless and humorless.

Yellow Submarine

Yellow Submarine (1968) is an animated adventure directed by George Dunning and Charles Jenkins, and produced by Al Brodax of King Features, the company behind the American *Beatles* cartoon show. The film is animated by George Dunning, Fred Wolf, Bob Balser, Eddie Radage, Charles Jenkins, and Jack Stokes, and designed by Heinz Edelmann with Dennis Rich. The screenplay is by Lee Minoff and Al Brodax with Jack Mendelsohn, Erich Segal (of *Love Story* fame), and Roger McGough (of McGear and McGough), from a story by Lee Minoff.

The voiceover cast includes John Clive as John, Geoff Hughes as Paul, Peter Batten as George, and Paul Angelis as Ringo. Distributed by United Artists. 85 minutes.

Yellow Submarine is only incidentally a Beatle movie; the Fabs had little to do with its production. It is also said that Brian Epstein agreed to it only because he believed that it would complete the Beatles' three-film deal with United Artists. To the dismay of all concerned, the UA deal required on-screen participation from the entire group.

Animated in classic late-1960s psychedelic style, the film is set in an undersea fantasy world. The plot involves an attack on Pepperland by an assortment of fantastical villains dedicated to the elimination of music, happiness, and love; these include the Blue Meanies, Apple Bonkers, Snapping Turtle Turks, and the snickering Flying Glove. The Beatles are summoned, board the famous banana-hued vehicle and pass through the Seas of Holes, Monsters, and Consumer Products on their way to the occupied city. Needless to say, in the end, love conquers all.

Unlike *A Hard Day's Night* and *Help!,* this third Beatle feature inspired very little musical activity aside from George Martin's orchestral score. Most of the Beatle songs are several years old, and the new recordings are mostly throwaways: "Hey Bulldog"—which appears only in the U.K. version of the film—had been churned out for the benefit of cameras shooting the MTV-style promo film for "Lady Madonna." "Only a Northern Song" betrays author George's cynicism in the title itself, a reference to the publishing company that owned his songs, but in which he had no ownership. "It's All Too Much" clearly is not given the band's most serious attention, and "All Together Now" may be the least substantial song the group ever recorded.

The critical reaction to the film was favorable, but the British public failed to catch on. In the U.S., however, *Yellow Submarine* was a great success.

Let It Be

Let It Be (1970) is a documentary directed by Michael Lindsay-Hogg, previously a director for the *Ready Steady Go!* television program, produced by Neil Aspinall, former Beatle road manager, and presented by Apple. The film stars John, Paul, George, and Ringo, with guest appearances by Yoko Ono, Billy Preston, Heather Eastman, George Martin, and Mal Evans. Distributed by United Artists. 88 minutes.

The final movie in the Beatles' deal with United Artists began as a rehearsal for their return to the concert stage after three eventful years, and ended as a meager consolation prize for fans in the wake of the group's breakup.

After the personality clashes that erupted during the White Album sessions, Paul devised a scheme to return the Beatles to their former state of cooperation and comradery: The band would rehearse for a series of concerts featuring all new material rather than tried and true hits, and the rehearsals would be filmed for a television documentary. The concerts would provide the prelude to a grand final show, preferably in an exotic location such as a Tunisian amphitheater, in the Sahara desert at sunrise, or in the middle of the ocean on a cruise ship. This climactic performance would be filmed for theatrical release, and recorded for release as the next Beatle album. The album would be packaged with a book of still photographs from the TV and feature films. Ideally, he planned for the record, book, TV special, and movie to be released simultaneously—a dramatic show of force from the Beatles, the undisputed pacesetters in music, hairstyles, clothing, and political opinion.

Paul booked the cavernous Twickenham Film Studio for the first two weeks of January 1969, summoned the Beatles, and hired a film crew. Twickenham, however, proved drafty, impersonal, and uninspiring, especially because the cameras peeped over the band members' shoulders from dawn until dusk. The other Beatles weren't sure they wanted to undertake the rigors of a tour; in fact, they weren't sure they wanted to perform at all. They couldn't decide whether they wanted to play old material or develop new songs. Tempers flared; at one point, George walked out on the band. He returned after a few days.

Facing growing resistance, Paul agreed to scale down the tour to a single concert, and finally, to an impromptu performance outdoors on the roof of Apple's offices. In order to record the album, the Beatles moved the production to their own studio, hastily assembled in the basement. The TV documentary and concert film condensed into a humble cinema-verité feature, provided a handy way of fulfilling the Beatles' obligation to supply United Artists with a successor to *Help!* and *A Hard Day's Night*.

In one month's time the Beatles generated ninety-six hours of film, from which director Michael Lindsay-Hogg was to create a documentary

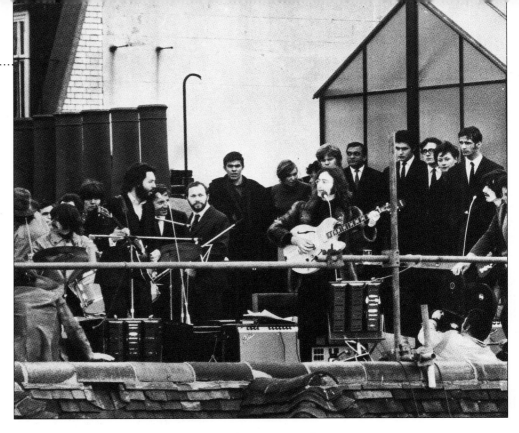

On the rooftop of Apple during the performance featured in *Let It Be*.

of the events. (Meanwhile, George Martin and engineer Glyn Johns were left with ninety-six hours of mono soundtrack and over thirty hours of multitrack tape, which contained take after take of the songs that would appear on the *Let It Be* album.)

Lindsay-Hogg's film was only partially successful. Despite a number of interesting moments—George's temper tantrum, the rooftop performance, the Beatles and Billy Preston's jam session in the Apple basement—the film fails to convey the significance of January 1969.

However, it does provide one piece of a puzzle that, when assembled, offers a unique window into the private world of the Beatles, and an opportunity to examine great artists at work that is, perhaps, entirely without parallel. When the official movie, record, and book are combined with sprawling archival remnants of film and tape that have surfaced in bootleg form, the picture is vivid indeed: four extraordinarily talented, desperately ambitious, and thoroughly weary artists who have reached the limit of a historic collaboration and must now carry on as individuals.

Let It Be met with a poor reception from both fans and the press. It did, however, win an Academy Award in 1970 for Best Original Song Score.

On the Apple Rooftop, the Beatles play: "Get Back," "Don't Let Me Down," "I've Got a Feeling," "One After 909," and "Dig a Pony."

In the studio, either in jam sessions or in properly rehearsed performances, the Beatles perform: "Piano Theme" (McCartney), "Don't Let Me Down," "Maxwell's Silver Hammer," "Two of Us," "I've Got a Feeling," "Oh! Darling," "One After 909," "Jazz Piano Song" (McCartney-Starkey), "Across the Universe," "Dig a Pony," "Suzy Parker" [as "Suzy's Parlor"] (Lennon-McCartney-Harrison-Starkey), "I Me Mine," "For You Blue," "Besame

Mucho" (Valazquez-Skylar), "Octopus' Garden," "You Really Got a Hold on Me" (Robinson), "The Long and Winding Road," "Shake, Rattle and Roll" (Calhoun), "Kansas City/Miss Ann/Lawdy Miss Clawdy" (Leiber-Stoller/Dolphy/Price), "Dig It," and "Let It Be."

Promotional Films

A very thin line separates MTV-style promotional films from appearances on U.K. television shows such as *Scene at 6:30*, *Thank Your Lucky Stars*, *Ready Steady Go!*, and *Top of the Pops* (in the U.S. *Hullabaloo* and *Shindig*). The bootleg video archive is full of such TV appearances, which are usually lip-synched simulations of a performance, sometimes with little pretense to realism. The Beatles apparently preferred this sort of presentation to the uncertainties of a live performance; on November 27, 1964, they became the first act to lip-synch on the exclusively live *Ready Steady Go!*

Later appearances, most notably the *David Frost Show* broadcast of "Hey Jude" (September 8, 1968) and the *Top of the Pops* version of "Revolution" (September 19, 1968), feature combinations of lip-synched and live vocals. Combining the two is said to have been a ploy to circumvent a Musicians Union's ban on mimed performances.

Nonetheless, many of the later clips, such as one that depicts the Fabs wandering around a botanical garden to the sound of "Rain"—presumably from the June 2, 1966 *Top of the Pops* show—are more like today's rock videos, which often feature action and imagery that have little to do with the song. Nonetheless, these clips technically are TV appearances, not promotional films.

According to Bill Harry's *Beatlemania: An Illustrated Filmography*, the first promotional film to be produced by the Beatles themselves is "Penny Lane." It was followed by "Strawberry Fields Forever," "Hello, Goodbye," and several others. None ever received widespread distribution, and some never made it to television at all.

The Beatles' final promotional clips ended up in the *Let It Be* movie; they were live-in-the-studio performances of "Two of Us," "The Long and Winding Road," and "Let It Be"; and they were shown on *The Ed Sullivan Show* on February 15, 1970.

These productions largely have been passed over by Beatle historians, and little information about them is readily available. The Beatles' promotional films, in chronological order, are:

"Penny Lane" (Lennon-**McCartney**)

The Beatles take a horseback ride through Liverpool. Filmed on January 30–31, 1967. Directed by Peter Goldmann. Debuted on *Top of the Pops* on February 9, 1967. Black and white.

"Strawberry Fields Forever"

(**Lennon**-McCartney)

A psychedelic extravaganza. The Beatles move through a mysterious landscape of color-reversed and -filtered scenery, often in slow motion or backward. Eventually, they overturn a piano whose strings are attached to a tall tree. Shot on February 5–7, 1967. Directed by Peter Goldmann. Debuted on *Top of the Pops* on February 9, 1967. Color.

"Hello, Goodbye" (Lennon-**McCartney**)

#1

The Beatles perform and horse around on a theatre stage in their brightly colored Sgt. Pepper suits. In one shot, you can see them in their collarless Pierre Cardin suits, circa 1964. Shot at the Saville Theatre on November 10, 1967. Directed by Paul McCartney. One of the three "Hello, Goodbye" films was debuted in the U.S. on *The Ed Sullivan Show*, November 26, 1967; the others may never have been broadcast. The Musicians Union ban on miming effectively killed the films in Britain. Color.

"Hello, Goodbye" (Lennon-**McCartney**)

#2

Similar to #1, except the band is wearing hippie clothing. Shot at the Saville Theatre on November 10, 1967. Directed by Paul McCartney. Color.

"Hello, Goodbye" (Lennon-**McCartney**)

#3

A mixture of shots in Sgt. Pepper suits and hippie clothes. There's a lot more fooling around in this edit. John and Paul do the Charleston and wink at the camera. George looks decidedly unconvinced that the whole thing is a good idea. The sight of the older, presumably wiser, and definitely more "psychedelic" Beatles recreating their Fab Four personalities is somewhat disconcerting. Shot at the Saville Theatre on November 10, 1967. Directed by Paul McCartney. Color.

"A Day in the Life"

(**Lennon**-McCartney)

A powerful film for a powerful song: An incoherent sequence of sped up, slowed down, unfocused, and double-exposed images are intercut at lightening speed, in sympathy with the dreamlike character of the music.

The footage, shot by Ringo with a hand-held camera, actually depicts the recording session for the song itself; a woman dressed in a flowing gown waves sparklers amidst an orchestra conducted by Paul and George Martin. As a demented touch, the musicians are wearing funny noses and masks; rather than comic relief, it only adds to the atmosphere of impending apocalypse. But the humor is allowed to shine through when a shot of Big Ben pops on at the sound of the alarm clock during Paul's segment of the song.

Mick Jagger, Marianne Faithful, Keith Richards, Donovan, Patti Boyd Harrison, and Mike Nesmith (of the Monkees) appear. Filmed at Abbey Road on February 10, 1967. Director unknown. According to Beatles assistant Tony Bramwell, the film was never broadcast in the U.K. due to a BBC ban on the song, which was thought to contain drug references. Color.

"Lady Madonna" (Lennon-**McCartney**)

The boys at work in the studio. Paul is at the piano, John is behind a microphone, George happily rocks away with his guitar, and Ringo pounds out the beat. They're actually recording "Hey, Bulldog," which was composed specifically for the shooting of this film so that the Beatles could make good use of the time they spent in the studio. Shot at Abbey Road on February 11, 1968. Director unknown. Debuted on *All Systems Freeman* (U.K.) on March 15, 1968. Color.

"Back in the USSR"

(Lennon-**McCartney**)

A compilation of Beatlemania-era welcome scenes as the Fabs touch down at various airports. Filmed circa 1964. Director and broadcast history unknown. Black and white.

"The Ballad of John and Yoko"

(**Lennon**-McCartney)

Debuted on *Music Scene* on September 22, 1969. No further information available.

"Something" (Harrison)

George's exquisite composition, which Frank Sinatra called "the best love song of the last fifty years," serves as a hook on which this film hangs shots of the four Beatles with their wives. For the most part, John and Yoko, Paul and Linda, George and Patti, and Ringo and Mo simply walk through fields or stare into each others' eyes. There are a few moments of action: Ringo and Mo hop on a pair of motorscooters, and Paul and Linda frolic with their sheepdog, Martha. For the most part the film is pure sentimentality, but oddly enough, the result is touching. Shooting date, director, and broadcast history unknown. Color.

"Don't Let Me Down"

(**Lennon**-McCartney)

Leftover footage from *Let It Be* is put to excellent use in this film, which intersperses scenes from Twickenham Studios and the Apple rooftop performance. The result would be right at home on MTV today. Filmed, in part, at Apple on January 30, 1969. Possibly directed by Michael Lindsay-Hogg (director of *Let It Be*). Broadcast history unknown.

The Fabs on BBC TV's *Top of the Pops*, June 16, 1966.

Commercial Video

A number of home-video releases are available for the Beatlemaniac who wants to spend an evening at home in front of the television. Most of the videos are spin-offs from television and feature film productions, although some, such as *The Compleat Beatles*, were conceived for video release. The following videography includes productions dealing directly with the Fab Four as a group. There are, of course, a multitude of other videos that involve individual Beatles (including Paul's rock videos, George's productions for Handmade Films, and Ringo's numerous star-turns).

TITLE	LABEL	CATALOG NUMBER	PRODUCTION DATE
Ready Steady Go!	Pioneer Artists, Inc.	87M053 (Laser Disc)	1963–4

Television compilation. Available in Laser Disc format only, this release collects several of the Beatles' *Ready Steady Go!* television appearances (available separately on videotape). 60 minutes.

Ready Steady Go!	HBO/Cannon Video	2195 (VHS, Beta)	1964
Volume 1	Pioneer Artists, Inc.	PA88198 (Laser Disc)	

Television compilation. This compilation of live *Ready Steady Go!* TV broadcasts collects appearances by various artists originally aired between March 20 and April 27, 1964. The Beatles perform "You Can't Do That" and "Can't Buy Me Love," followed by Cilla Black, Them, the Animals, Gerry and the Pacemakers, the Who, the Rolling Stones, and others. 57 minutes.

Ready Steady Go!	HBO/Cannon Video	2377 (VHS, Beta)	1963
Volume 2	Pioneer Artists, Inc.	PA88217 (Laser Disc)	

Television compilation. The Beatles segment includes live performances of "She Loves You" and "Twist and Shout" culled from *Ready Steady Go!* broadcast on October 4, 1963. Other featured artists include the Beach Boys and the Rolling Stones. 55 minutes.

Ready Steady Go!	HBO/Cannon Video	3352 (VHS, Beta)	1964
Volume 3			

Television compilation. The Beatles perform "Baby's in Black," "She's a Woman," and "Kansas City/Hey, Hey, Hey, Hey" from the live broadcast of *Ready Steady Go!* on November 27, 1964. Marvin Gaye and the Rolling Stones also perform. 57 minutes.

The Beatles Live	Sony Video Software	97W50093 (VHS)	1964
		97W00092 (Beta, 8mm)	

Television special/concert (excerpts). This video includes excerpts from lip-synched performances originally aired as part of the BBC's one-hour special *Around the Beatles* in May 1964. The Beatles perform "Twist and Shout," "Roll Over Beethoven," "I Wanna Be Your Man," "Long Tall Sally," and a brief medley of current hits, as well as a rare rendition of "Shout" (Isley-Isley-Isley). 20 minutes.

A Hard Day's Night	MPI Home Video	1064 (VHS, Beta, Laser Disc)	1964
	Criterion/Voyager	CC1175 L (Laser Disc)	

Feature. 90 minutes.

Criterion's special edition, available only in Laser Disc format, includes the theatrical trailer for the film, an interview with director Richard Lester, and Lester's initial success, *The Running, Jumping, Standing Still Film* (comedy, 1959) in its entirety. 200 minutes.

See chapter five, "The Beatles on Film: Feature Films," p. 102.

Help!	MPI Home Video	1342 (VHS, Beta)	1965
	Criterion	2004L (Laser Disc)	

Feature. 90 minutes.

Criterion's special edition, available only in Laser Disc format, includes behind-the-scenes footage, coverage of the film's world premiere, and survey of memorabilia. 105 minutes.

See chapter five, "The Beatles on Film: Feature Films," p. 104.

Magical Mystery Tour	Media Home Entertainment	M430 (VHS, Beta)	1967
	MPI Home Video	1538 (VHS, Beta)	1967

Television special/feature. 50 minutes.

Media Home Entertainment released the original home-video issue of the film.

MPI's version is newly remastered. Its look and sound are far superior to those of the other issues.

See chapter five, "The Beatles on Film: Feature Films," p. 104.

See chapter three, "The Beatles on Record: Selected LP and CD Releases," p. 67.

Yellow Submarine	MGM/UA Home Video	M301170 (VHS, Beta)	1968

Feature. 85 minutes.

See "The Beatles on Film: Feature Films," p. 105.

Let It Be	CBS/Fox Video	4508 (VHS, Beta)	1969
	RCA Selectavision	01411 (Capacitance Disc)	

Documentary. 113 minutes.

See chapter five, "The Beatles on Film: Feature Films," p. 106.

See chapter three, "The Beatles on Record: Selected LP and CD Releases," p. 72.

The Compleat Beatles	MGM/UA Home Video	MV700166 (VHS)	1982
		M700166 (Beta)	
		Available on Laser Disc.	

Documentary. This 1982 production presents an excellent chronological overview of the Beatles influences, music, and career, and was produced to accompany the book of the same name.

Made specifically for video release, the feature-length production includes a wealth of interviews and archival footage. A history of skiffle and Merseybeat, complete with stylistic demonstrations by Gerry Marsden (of Gerry and the Pacemakers), provides a solid background for Beatle history.

Other highlights include the Cavern Club performance of "Some Other Guy" (Lieber-Stoller-Barrett) filmed on August 22, 1962, by Granada Television and interviews with Tony Sheridan, Horst Fascher, and George Martin. Rare clips such as the *Our World* broadcast of "All You Need Is Love" are an added attraction. 120 minutes.

Ringo takes the camera during the filming of *Help!*

The Beatles in Print: A Selected Bibliography

Books
General History

Bacon, David and Norman Maslov. *The Beatles' England: There Are Places I'll Remember.* London: Columbus Books, 1982.
  Geographical survey of the Fabs' stomping grounds.

Baker, Glenn A. *The Beatles Down Under: The 1964 Australia and New Zealand Tour.* Ann Arbor: Popular Culture, Ink., 1982.
  Vivid treatment of an otherwise lost period in Beatle history, including Jimmy Nichol's short stand-in for Ringo.

Blake, John. *All You Needed Was Love: The Beatles After the Beatles.* New York: Putnam's/Perigee Books, 1981.
  Often rivaling a supermarket tabloid in tone, this is nonetheless one of the few books available that covers the post-Beatle fortunes of John, Paul, and George in any depth. Ringo makes cameo appearances.

Cepican, Bob and Waleed Ali. *Yesterday... Came Suddenly.* New York: Arbor House, 1985.
  Another history covering the fortunes of the four ex-Beatles.

Davies, Hunter. *The Beatles: The Authorized Biography (Second Revised Edition).* New York: McGraw-Hill, 1985.
  The original biography, which was so thoroughly neutered by Brian Epstein, Mimi Stanley, and others on its way to publication that John called it "crap," has been updated to treat events more frankly. The new edition includes a postscript on each Fab.

Above: On *The Ed Sullivan Show*, 1964. Opposite, top: Paul phones home to England from the set of *Help!* Opposite, bottom: The Fab Four (circa 1965).

De Witt, Howard A. *The Beatles: Untold Tales.* Fremont, CA: Horizon Books, 1985.
  A detailed examination of the era in which the early Beatles rose to prominence. The prose lacks excitement, but the content is rewarding.

Evans, Mike and Ron Jones. *In the Footsteps of the Beatles.* Liverpool: Merseyside County Council, 1981.
  Geographic overview of the Beatles' home town.

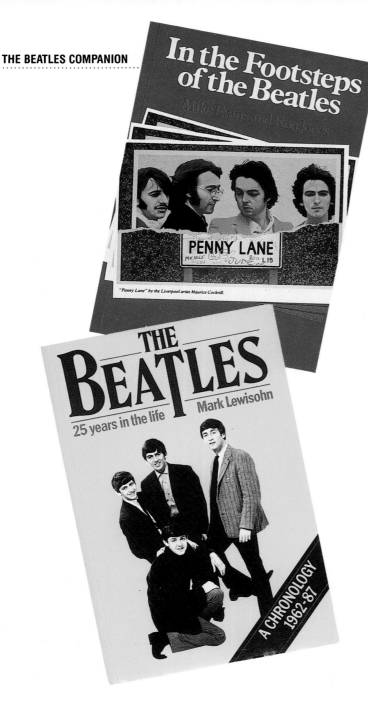

Liverpool, City of. *The Beatles Collection.* Liverpool: City of Liverpool Public Relations Dept., 1975.

Deluxe LP-sized package containing maps, a discography, a history book, and other items of interest.

McCabe, Peter and Robert Schonfeld. *Apple to the Core: The Unmaking of the Beatles.* London: Martin Brian and O'Keefe, 1972.

McCabe and Schonfeld's capsule history of the years leading up to the founding of Apple is one of the best brief histories you'll find. The focus of the book, however, is on Apple. In attempting to lay bare the Beatles' labyrinthine business entanglements, the authors unfortunately fail to convey a clear sense of what happened. On the other hand, no one has written a better book on the subject. Ultimately, this book's contribution to Beatle history is its compelling argument that Allen Klein and Lee Eastman, not Paul, John, or Yoko, broke up the Beatles.

Norman, Philip. *Shout! The Beatles in Their Generation.* New York: Simon and Schuster, 1981.

Well-documented, intricately detailed, and as gripping as a novel, Norman's history is an easy contender for the best history on the group ever written. Essential.

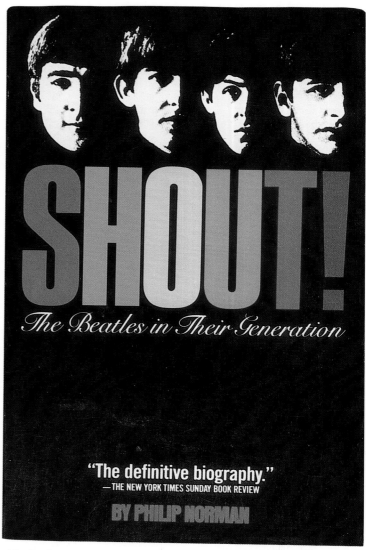

Friede, Goldie, Robin Titone, and Sue Weiner. *The Beatles A to Z.* New York: Methuen, Inc., 1980.

A Fab Four encyclopedia. Skimpy on information, but useful as a collection of interesting topics worth looking into further.

Harry, Bill. *The Beatles Who's Who.* New York: Delilah Books, 1982.

If anyone should know who's who, it's Bill Harry. One of the furthest inside of the "insiders," Harry founded *Mersey Beat*, arguably the first local music rag. He was a close friend of the Fabs, and instrumental in making them Liverpool's top band.

Harry's books, while not the most factually accurate, carry with them the authority of someone who was utterly dedicated to the Liverpool music scene. This is his roundup of important people in the Beatles' career. He tells the Beatles' story in a series of thumbnail profiles.

Leigh, Spenser. *Let's Go Down the Cavern: The Story of Liverpool's Mersey-beat.* London: Vermillion Books, 1984.

History of the Liverpool club where the Beatles were the house band.

Lewisohn, Mark. *The Beatles Day by Day: A Chronology, 1962-1989* (revised edition; original title: *The Beatles: Twenty-Five Years in the Life, 1962-1987*) New York: Harmony Books, 1990.

A concise chronology, and guaranteed—as with all of Lewisohn's books—to be the most authoritative on the market.

The Beatles continue to inspire a wide variety of reading material, from biographies and official studio session notes to discographies and fanzines.

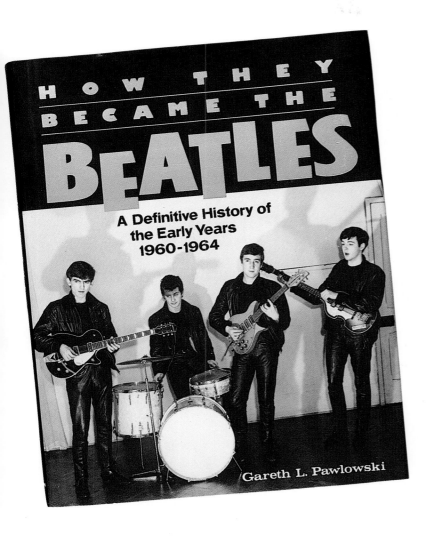

Okun, Milton, ed. *The Compleat Beatles, Volumes 1 and 2.* New York: Delilah/ATV/Bantam, 1981.

Sheet music, reportage, criticism, history, reminiscences, photographs, and trivia all rolled into two deluxe volumes.

Pawlowski, Gareth L. *How They Became the Beatles: A Definitive History of the Early Years, 1960-1964.* New York: E. P. Dutton, 1989.

Never mind that the text is devoted entirely to the Fabs' underreported Liverpool period—it's the illustrations that make this book a must-have. Gorgeous reproductions of concert posters, personal letters, record labels, newspaper articles, contracts, and other such documents are set amidst the most extensive collection of early photographs ever published. This is the first book to provide a visual context for the Mersey scene comparable to the now-familiar imagery of the Beatlemania years.

Schaffner, Nicholas. *The Beatles Forever.* Harrisburg, PA: Cameron House, 1977.

Written and designed with well-informed enthusiasm as well as "insider" access, this is generally regarded as one of the best Beatle histories.

Schultheiss, Tom. *A Day in the Life: The Beatles Day by Day, 1960-1970.* Ann Arbor: Popular Culture, Ink., 1980.

The most exhaustive chronology available, it details the Beatles' lives in excruciating detail.

Southall, Brian. *Abbey Road.* Cambridge: Patrick Stephens, Ltd., 1982.

Official history of the recording studio made famous by the Beatles.

Memoirs

It's interesting to note that the Beatle-related memoirs are often the least accurate Beatles' texts from a factual point of view—events are reported out of sequence, names misremembered, motives misattributed. As Castleman and Podrazik point out in *The Beatles Again,* "very often the worst source of information is someone who was there at the time!"

On the other hand, a personalized account, unlike the more objective historical book, can convey an experiential context that can be far more truthful in its essential character than any assemblage of raw data, and provide unique insight into the personalities behind the events. When combined with more objective accounts, the books listed below fill out the Beatles' story in all of its larger-than-life drama.

Baird, Julia. *John Lennon, My Brother: Memories of Growing Up Together.* New York: Henry Holt and Co., 1988.

John was six years old when his half-sister Julia Dykins (now Baird) was born. This book describes how his life affected hers.

Bedford, Carol. *Waiting for the Beatles.* Poole, Dorset: Blandford Press, 1984.

A firsthand account of the experiences of an Apple Scruff, one of a core group of fans who spent years hovering around the doors to Apple, Abbey Road, and the Fabs' homes.

Best, Pete and Patrick Doncaster. *Beatle! The Pete Best Story.* London: Plexus Publishing, 1985.

The story of Best's struggle to avoid becoming the Beatle that time forgot.

Brown, Peter and Stephen Gaines. *The Love You Make: An Insider's Story of the Beatles.* New York: McGraw-Hill, 1983.

Peter Brown, at one time Brian Epstein's assistant and later an Apple executive, witnessed the rise and fall of the Fabs firsthand.

DiLello, Richard. *The Longest Cocktail Party: An Insider's Diary of the Beatles, Their Million-Dollar Apple Empire and Its Wild Rise and Fall.* Ann Arbor: Popular Culture, Ink., 1972.

An entertaining peek inside of Apple Corps. from the company's official "House Hippie." This book seems to have become one of the primary sources of information about the Beatles' most ambitious project.

Epstein, Brian. *A Cellarful of Noise.* Ann Arbor: Popular Culture, Ink., 1964.

An early autobiography of the man who discovered the Beatles, and so successfully packaged them for public consumption. As Merseyside author Bill Harry observed, this book gives the reader the impression that Epstein created the Merseyside scene single-handedly, which he didn't. He did, however, bring the "Mersey Beat" to international attention and gave it a place in the history of popular music.

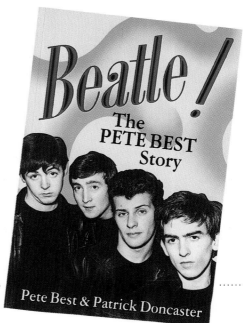

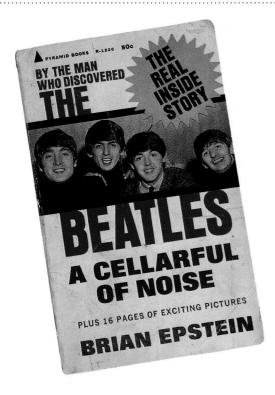

Kaufman, Murray. *Murray the K Tells It Like It Is, Baby.* New York: Holt, Rinehart and Winston, 1966.

Amidst the chaos of Beatlemania in the U.S. circa 1964, New York DJ Murray the K schmoozed his way into the Beatles' hotel room and managed to interview them on the air via telephone before Brian Epstein broke up the party. He accompanied them on tour in 1964 and 1965, and became particularly close to George, who wrote the foreword to this autobiography.

Lennon, Cynthia. *A Twist of Lennon.* London: Star Books/W. H. Allen, 1978.
A prim and retiring reminiscence by John's first wife.

Martin, George with Jeremy Hornsby. *All You Need Is Ears: The Inside, Personal Story of the Genius Who Created the Beatles.* New York: St. Martin's Press, 1979.

Happily, Martin makes no claim within these pages that he "created the Beatles." He simply tells the story of how an amateur composer, employed by a backwater division of EMI, became the most respected record producer in the business.

Schwartz, Francie. *Body Count.* San Francisco: Straight Arrow Books, 1972.
The kiss-and-tell account of an American would-be screenwriter who came to Apple to peddle a script and became Paul's lover instead.

Shotton, Pete. *John Lennon: In My Life.* New York: Stein and Day, 1983.
A pal during John's childhood, his first musical collaborator during adolescence, and one of the critical links in his support system as an adult, Pete Shotton was perhaps closer to John than anyone beside Yoko. His memories are vastly entertaining.

Taylor, Derek. *As Time Goes By: Living in the Sixties.* Ann Arbor: Pierian Press, 1973.

Taylor, a publicist of NEMS Enterprises, and later Apple, is the most consistently engaging commentator on the Beatles and their milieu. In a droll, run-on style he recounts the cheerful insanity that drew him alternately into and out of the Beatles' inner circle.

——. *Fifty Years Adrift (In an Open-Necked Shirt).* Guilford, Surrey: Genesis, 1985.

For the literate Beatlemaniac: leather-bound and limited to only 2,000 copies, edited and annotated by George.

Williams, Allan and William Marshall. *The Man Who Gave the Beatles Away.* London: Elm Tree/Hamilton, 1975.

Paul McCartney has called this book "a work of fiction," and Bill Harry—who should know—finds little in it that rings true to him. Williams never "had" the Beatles to "give them away"; he gave them opportunities, reluctantly by most accounts, at a few key moments in their career. Nonetheless, this is one man's view of the Beatles' rise to the top.

Musical History

Carr, Ron and Tony Tyler. *The Beatles: An Illustrated Record.* New York: Harmony Books, 1981.

Flashy, large-format book packed with information and photographs—basic history and discography that's also fun to look at.

Dowlding, William J. *Beatlesongs.* New York: Fireside/Simon and Schuster, 1989.

An interesting attempt to draw together, song by song, quotations by the Beatles and historical information about the writing, performing, recording, and marketing of each composition. Dowlding relies heavily on too few sources, some of questionable accuracy, and stops short of attempting to reveal and resolve conflicting accounts. Nonetheless, very useful and entertaining.

Howlett, Kevin. *The Beatles at the Beeb: The Story of Their Radio Career, 1962–1965.* Ann Arbor: Popular Culture, Ink., 1982.

Definitive chronicle of the BBC broadcasts, complete with transcriptions of the more entertaining exchanges between the DJs and the Fabs.

King, L.R.E. *Help! A Companion to The Beatles Recording Sessions.* Tucson: Storyteller Productions, 1988.

King organizes the recording session chronology from Lewisohn's book *The Beatles Recording Sessions* on a song-by-song basis, which provides an at-a-glance view of the recording history of each composition. Very handy.

Lewisohn, Mark. *The Beatles Live!* New York: Pavillion Books, 1985.
The only book to examine the Beatles strictly as a performing ensemble. Lewisohn lists every Quarry Men/Moondogs/Beatles concert that he has been able to document, from obscure dates at the Jacaranda Club to the stadium shows of the later tours, and adds well-informed commentary along the way. Each year's list of performances is accompanied by a catalog of songs in the group's repertoire, including such buried treasures as "Looking Glass" (Lennon-McCartney) and "Thinking of Linking" (Lennon-McCartney). In the case of songs by other composers, he even pinpoints the rendition on which the Beatles based their arrangement. An astonishing work of scholarship, and a treasure trove of information and anecdotes for even the most casual fan.

——. *The Beatles Recording Sessions: The Official Abbey Road Studio Session Notes, 1962–1970.* New York: Harmony Books, 1988.

Another essential book from Lewisohn. This book is a great deal of fun because you can listen to the records as you read about how they were made. Given access to the complete EMI tape library, Lewisohn has constructed a comprehensive log of the Fab Four's recording sessions at Abbey Road, and details the results of each one. For the first time, you can follow the development of a complex recording such as "Strawberry Fields Forever" from unfinished tracks to rough mixes to abandoned arrangements to the finished product. In addition, the book is chock-full of anecdotes from EMI personnel and session players, and photographs of the Beatles at work in the studio. *The Beatles Recording Sessions* is truly the next best thing to being in the studio with the Fab Four.

Musicology and Music Criticism

Mellers, Wilfrid. *Twilight of the Gods: The Music of the Beatles.* New York: Schirmer/Macmillan, 1975.

Mellers is the leader in academic-style criticism of the Beatles' work. He analyzes the harmonic, melodic, rhythmic, and stylistic structures of the entire Beatles repertoire to discover what makes the music so effective. His conclusions are often obscure, always entertaining, and sometimes illuminating.

Discography

Castleman, Harry and Walter Podrazik. *All Together Now: The First Complete Beatles Discography 1961–1975.* Ann Arbor: Popular Culture, Ink., 1975.

The first of three extensive discographies (see below), all of which are comprehensively indexed in the final volume, *The End of the Beatles?* For official releases, this is the essential source. Films, books, conventions, and other topics are also covered, but in less detail.

With the publication of *All Together Now*, Pierian Press of Ann Arbor, Michigan established itself as the provider of the best in scholarly literature on the Fab Four. They went on to publish an outstanding catalog of titles, and also picked up a few out-of-print items such as Beatle publicist Derek Taylor's *As Time Goes By*. The company's Beatles catalog recently passed into the hands of Popular Culture, Ink. (Box 1839, Ann Arbor, MI 48106), headed by Fab chronologist Tom Schultheiss.

———. *The Beatles Again.* Ann Arbor: Popular Culture, Ink., 1977.

———. *The End of the Beatles?* Ann Arbor: Popular Culture, Ink., 1985.

Cox, Perry and Michael Miller. *The Beatles Price and Reference Guide for American Records.* Phoenix: Cox-Miller, 1986.

For serious collectors. This guide includes every Beatles record released in the U.S., including label variations, cover variations, rereleases, compilations, charity gigs, and all types of oddball vinyl.

King, L.R.E. *Do You Want to Know a Secret? Making Sense of the Beatles' Unreleased Recordings.* Tucson: Storyteller Productions, 1988.

The Beatle bootleg bible. King verifies the contents of hundreds of unauthorized releases, and specifies correct song titles, songwriting credits, dates, venues, and other points of fact, regardless of what's printed on the album sleeve. As an added bonus, special chapters cover Liverpool-era recordings, the *Get Back/Let It Be* project, the aborted *Sessions* album, BBC broadcasts, and recordings that remain unissued in any form. An invaluable resource for anyone interested in bootlegs.

———. *Fixing a Hole: A Second Look at the Beatles' Unauthorized Recordings.* Tucson: Storyteller Productions, 1989.

More of the same in what King promises will be a three-volume series.

Levy, Jeffrey. *Apple Log IV: A Guide for the U.S. and Canadian Apple Records Collector.* Ottawa: MonHunProd Media Group, 1990.

A comprehensive Apple discography, illustrated with picture sleeves, labels, and historic print ads for Apple releases.

McCoy, William and Mitchell McGeary. *Every Little Thing: The Definitive Guide to Beatles Recording Variations, Rare Mixes and Other Musical Oddities, 1958–1986.* Ann Arbor: Popular Culture, Ink., 1990.

Oddly enough, one issue of a given song isn't necessarily the same as the next. How many versions of "I'm Only Sleeping" are there? If you're really sure you want to know, this book will tell you.

Reinhart, Charles. *You Can't Do That: Beatles Bootlegs and Novelty Records, 1963–1980.* Ann Arbor: Popular Culture, Ink., 1981.

The first attempt to catalog bootlegs and their contents (over eight hundred of 'em)—including a huge number of records not covered in L.R.E. King's books. The state of Beatle scholarship has come a long way since Reinhart's book was published, so much of the information is no longer as accurate as it could be. However, *You Can't Do That* remains essential for its roundup of Beatle counterfeits, satires, tributes, cheap imitations, and other legitimate Beatle-related disks.

Russell, Jeff. *The Beatles Album File and Complete Discography* (U.S. title: *The Beatles on Record: A Listener's Guide.*) Poole, Dorset: Blanford Press, 1982.

Fan-oriented discussion of legitimate releases, with a short essay about nearly every song.

Schwartz, David. *Listening to the Beatles: An Audiophile's Guide to the Sound of the Fab Four, Volume 1: Singles.* Ann Arbor: Popular Culture, Ink., 1990.

Evaluation of the sound of different releases of the Beatle catalog, with an effort to determine the "best-sounding" issue.

Stannard, Neville. *The Long and Winding Road: A History of the Beatles on Record.* London: Virgin Books, 1982.

A well-researched annotated discography of official releases, along with some bootlegs and novelties.

Stannard, Neville and John Tobler. *Working Class Heroes: The History of the Beatles' Solo Recordings.* London: Virgin Books, 1983.

Stannard and Tobler chronicle the Beatles' solo releases.

Wallgren, Mark. *The Beatles on Record.* New York: Fireside/Simon and Schuster, 1982.

Another highly regarded annotated discography of official releases.

Wiener, Allen J. *The Beatles: A Recording History.* Jefferson, NC: McFarland and Co., 1986.

Arranged as a series of exhaustive chronologies, Wiener's book covers general history, official releases, bootlegs, limited-circulation releases, unreleased recordings, alternate versions, and other topics.

Filmography

Harry, Bill. *Beatlemania: An Illustrated Filmography.* London: Virgin Books, 1984.

Harry's approach is usually a little lax when it comes to names and dates, but this remains the only reference for Beatle TV and film appearances.

Bibliography

Harry, Bill. *Paperback Writers: An Illustrated Bibliography.* London: Virgin Books, 1984.

Very useful annotated roundup of books about the Fab Four.

Terry, Carol D. *Here, There and Everywhere: The First International Beatles Bibliography, 1962–1982.* Ann Arbor: Popular Culture, Ink., 1985.

Serious bibliography, containing virtually every Beatle-related book, newspaper article, magazine feature, record review, or sheet music publication the author could dig up. Not recommended for light reading.

Literary Compilations and Criticism

Campbell, Colin and Allan Murphy. *Things We Said Today: The Complete Lyrics and a Concordance to the Beatles' Songs, 1962-1970.* Ann Arbor: Popular Culture, Ink., 1980.

Following in the footsteps of scholars of Shakespeare and the Bible, the authors have determined the location, frequency, and usage of every word that appears on a Beatle record. Astonishing.

Catone, Marc A., ed. *As I Write This Letter: An American Generation Remembers the Beatles.* Ann Arbor: Popular Culture, Ink., 1982.

A book for fans by fans. Via advertisements in newspapers and magazines, the editor invited people to write about what the Fabs had meant to them.

The Complete Beatles Lyrics. London: Omnibus Press, 1982.

Harry, Bill. *Mersey Beat: The Beginnings of the Beatles.* London: Omnibus Press, 1977.

A collection of Beatle-related clippings from Harry's groundbreaking Liverpool arts and entertainment rag, it includes John's regular "Beatcomber" columns.

Neises, Charles P., ed. *The Beatles Reader: A Selection of Contemporary Views, News and Reviews of the Beatles in Their Heyday.* Ann Arbor: Popular Culture, Ink., 1984.

Essays drawn from periodicals, including articles by David Fast, William F. Buckley, and Jonathan Cott, among others.

Collectors' References

Augsburger, Jeff, Marty Eck, and Rick Rann. *The Beatles Memorabilia Price Guide.* Elburn, IL: Branyan Press, 1988.

A beautifully illustrated catalog of Beatle-related material culture.

Fenick, Barbara. *Collecting the Beatles: An Introduction and Price Guide to Fab Four Collectibles, Records, and Memorabilia, Volumes 1 and 2.* Ann Arbor: Popular Culture, Ink., 1982.

Fenick edits *The Write Thing*, a fanzine for collectors of memorabilia, so she knows her stuff.

Photographs

Evans, Mike. *The Art of the Beatles.* London: Anthony Blond/Muller, Blond, and White Ltd., 1984.

More than a book of photographs, this is a collection of Beatles iconography: album covers, fashions, design, sculpture. This is Beatlemania in its visual manifestations.

Freeman, Robert. *Yesterday: Photographs of the Beatles.* London: Weidenfeld and Nicholson, 1983.

Midperiod photos from the man who shot the covers of *Beatles for Sale* and *Rubber Soul.*

Hoffman, Dezo. *The Beatles Conquer America: The Photographic Record of Their First Tour.* London: Virgin Books, 1984.

Portraits from the era of the clean-cut Beatle image.

——. *With the Beatles.* London: Omnibus Press, 1982.

More from Hoffman, shot between 1962 and 1965.

Parkinson, Norman and Maureen Cleave. *The Beatle Book.* London: Hutchinson, 1964.

High-quality shots by a top commercial photographer (Parkinson), annotated by the reporter (Cleave) who coaxed John into stating his thoughts about organized religion.

Russell, Ethan, Jonathan Cott, and David Dalton. *The Beatles Get Back.* London: Apple Publishing, 1969.

Russell's stills from the *Get Back/Let It Be* sessions, annotated with Cott and Dalton's transcriptions of conversations among the Fabs.

Stokes, Geoffrey. *The Beatles.* New York: Times Books/Rolling Stone, 1981.

The ultimate Fab Four coffee-table book, it offers portraits from a number of premier photographers including Richard Avedon.

Vollmer, Jurgen. *Rock'n'Roll Times: The Style and Spirit of the Early Beatles and Their First Fans.* New York: Google Plex Books, 1981.

Vollmer was a friend of Klaus Voorman and Astrid Kirchherr's in Hamburg; they brought him along to see the Beatles at the Kaiserkeller in 1961. Along with Kirchherr's, his photographs best document the Hamburg scene. One of Vollmer's portraits became the cover of John's *Rock'n'Roll* [CD: Parlophone/EMI CDP 7 46707 2 (1975)].

Trivia

Harry, Bill. *The Book of Beatle Lists.* Poole, Dorset: Javelin Books, 1985.

Lists covering every imaginable Beatle topic, from birthdays to chart-toppers.

Hockinson, Michael J. *Nothing is Beatleproof: Advanced Beatle Trivia for Fab Four Fanciers.* Ann Arbor: Popular Culture, Ink., 1990.

Fanzines

Generally, the people who write for fanzines are fans before they're professionals. Their work tends to be a labor of love. Not only do they take a refreshingly personal approach, they also cultivate sources of information that other publications tend to overlook: Beatle family members, former Beatle employees, collectors, convention organizers, and of course other hard-core fans. In a fanzine you'll find details that would be considered too obscure for a mainstream publication: first-hand reports, unreleased songs, tour schedules, favorite colors—you name it.

The publications listed below are dedicated to the Beatles as a whole. There are also fanzines devoted to John, Paul, George, and Ringo as individuals—not to mention Yoko Ono, Jane Asher, and other non-Beatles whose association with the Fabs has earned them a cult following.

Most fanzines aren't high-finance ventures. Some do feature exclusive full-color photographs printed on glossy paper, but many are produced by using a xerox machine and a stapler. Many fanzines operate on an issue-by-issue basis and don't appear again until enough material (or inspiration) is available to justify a new issue. Even the most humble of these, however, will prove enjoyable and valuable to a true Beatlemaniac.

Beatlefan [bimonthly]
The Goody Press
Box 33515
Decatur, GA 30033
    Slick and professional. Glossy cover, ample page count, a large amount of news, informed reviews, and relevant articles. One of the more substantial fanzines.

The Beatles Beat Downunder
P.O. Box 303
Magill 5072 S.A.
Australia
    Published quarterly. A lively fanzine with plenty of Fab facts and photos.

The Beatles Book [monthly]
Beat Publications Ltd.
45 St. Mary's Road
Ealing, London W5 5RQ
England
    An outgrowth of the original Beatles Fan Club publication, *The Beatles Book* resumed publication in the early 1980s with reprints of the original issues, and continues with new material to this day. Today, it's glossy, well-written, full of news, and packed with exclusive color photographs.

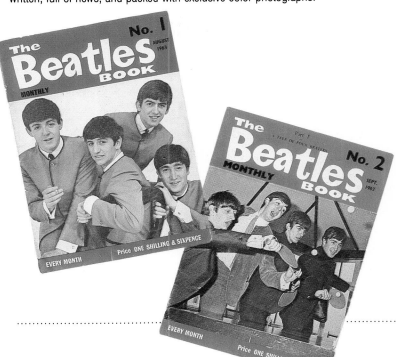

Beatles Now [bimonthly]
33 The Avenue
Highams Park, London E4 9LB
England
    Short on content compared with the usual fanzine, but generally a classier production, it features glossy, heavy-stock paper, and is packed with unique color photos.

The Beatles Records Information Service
P.O. Box 6
Dec Why 2099
New South Wales, Australia
    Doesn't publish a fanzine, but responds to queries.

Beatles Unlimited [bimonthly]
Box 602
3430 AP Nieuwegein
The Netherlands
    Impeccably designed and authoritatively reported, this is Beatlemania with a European touch of class. The record and book reviews are oriented toward fact rather than opinion.

The Beatletter [quarterly]
Box 13
St. Clair Shores, MI 48080
    Definitive factual information about new releases geared toward serious collectors.

Belmo's Beatleg News [bimonthly]
Storyteller Productions
Box 77513
Tucson, AZ 85703
    An excellent source of information about bootleg releases, new and old. Regular reviews, occasional features, and fine-tooth-comb examinations, often via the letters column, of bootleg origins.

F.A.B.: Fanatic About Beatles [quarterly]
Wow Ink
Box 4197
College Point, NY 11356
    Very detailed news coverage, reviews, and a crossword puzzle.

Good Day Sunshine [bimonthly]
Liverpool Productions
397 Edgewood Avenue
New Haven, CT 06511-4013
    News, articles, reminiscences, press conference transcripts, and exclusive photos, delivered with a personal touch. Usually more pages than your average fanzine.

The 910 [bimonthly]
Box 133
Cliffwood, NJ 07721
    An exhaustive source of information about Fab bootleg recordings, including reviews of new releases. Feature articles delve into technical and musicological insights to be gleaned from bootlegs.

The Write Thing [quarterly]
Box 18807
Minneapolis, MN 55418
    Editor Barbara Fenick has penned the definitive guides to Beatle memorabilia, *Collecting the Beatles*. Oriented toward collectors, this publication also includes news and fan reminiscences.

INDEX

Song titles are listed in quotation marks. Album titles are in italics. Titles of promotional films, full-length movies, and video cassettes are noted in parentheses. Names of authors are in parentheses following the book title.

A

Abbey Road, 22, 31, 41
  songs on, 70
Acetates, 86–89
"Across the Universe," 89
"Act Naturally," 60
After the Hurricane: Songs for Montserrat, 41
"Ain't She Sweet," 40, 44, 54
Alfie (movie), 36
All My Loving, songs on, 56
All Our Loving, 85
All-Starr Band, 26
All Things Must Pass, 22, 41
All You Need Is Ears (Martin), 41
"All You Need Is Love," 66
"And I Love Her," 55
Andrews, Bernie, 40
Another Beatles Christmas Record, 82
Apple Corps Ltd., 13
Apple to the Core (McCabe and Schonfeld), 38
Arias, Olivia Trinidad, 32
Asher, Jane, 36
Asher, Peter, 36
"Ask Me Why," 48
Aspinall, Neil, 37, 42

B

"Baby, You're a Rich Man," 66
Bach, Barbara, 26, 32
Back in the USSR (film), 106
"Back in the USSR," 26
Back to the Egg, 30
"Bad to Me," 88
Ballad of John and Yoko, The (film), 106
"Ballad of John and Yoko, The," 37, 71
Band on the Run, 18
Barrow, Tony, 37, 41
Beach Boys, 39
Beatles' Christmas Album, The, 83
Beatles' First, The, songs on, 51
Beatles' Fourth Christmas Record, The: Pantomime: Everywhere It's Christmas, 82

Beatles' Hits, The, songs on, 49
Beatles' Million Sellers, The, songs on, 62
Beatles' Movie Medley, The, 81
Beatles' Second Album, The, songs on, 50
Beatles, The (No. 1), songs on, 49
Beatles '65, The, songs on, 53
Beatles' Third Christmas Record, The, 82
Beatles 1968 Christmas Record, The, 83
Beatles at Shea Stadium, The (movie), 104
Beatles Box, The, 77
Beatles Christmas Record, The, 82
Beatles Collection, The, 76
Beatles EP Collection, The, songs on, 81
Beatles for Sale, songs on, 52, 61
Beatles Historic Sessions, The, 78
Beatles Live, The (video), 108
Beatles Live at the Hollywood Bowl, The, songs on, 75
Beatles Live at the Washington Coliseum, The (movie), 104
Beatlesongs (Dowlding), 42
Beatles Seventh Christmas, The, 83
Beatles Singles Collection, The, 81
Beatles Story, The, 84
Beatles Talking About . . ., 86
Beatles Tapes from the David Wigg Interviews, The, 86
Beatles VI, songs on, 58
Beatles with Yoko Ono, The, 89
Beatles Yesterday and Today, The, songs on, 62
Beatle! The Pete Best Story (Best), 30
"Be-Bop-A-Lula," 14
"Because," 14
Beck, Jeff, 41
Bee Gees, 39
"Being for the Benefit of Mr. Kite," 41
Best, Mona, 30
Best, Pete, 10, 26, 30, 31, 37, 39, 40
Beyond the Fringe (movie), 41
Black, Cilla, 37, 39
Black Jacks, 30
Blow by Blow, 41
Boyd, Patricia Anne, 30, 32
Brideshead Revisited (TV show), 36
Brown, Ken, 30
Brown, Peter, 37, 38
"Bungalow Bill," 32
Business associates, 37–39
Byrds, 39
Byrne, Nicky, 37

C

"Can't Buy Me Love," 53
Candy (movie), 26
Capitol Records, distribution agreement with, 10
Captain Beefheart, 39
Cass and the Cassanovas, 31
Caveman (movie), 26
Cellarful of Noise, A (Epstein and Taylor), 39
Cher, 41
Christmas records, 82–83
Christmas Time Is Here Again!, 82
Cicadelic Records, 85–86
Clapton, Eric, 22, 30, 32
Clemons, Clarence, 26
Cloud Nine, 22
Coleman, Ornette, 35
Coleman, Syd, 37, 38
Collection of Beatle Oldies, A, songs on, 63
"Come Together," 71
Compleat Beatles, The (video), 109
Complete Silver Beatles, The, songs on, 78
Concert for Bangladesh, The, 22, 41
Cooke, Sam, 38
Cooler, The (movie), 32
Costello, Elvis, 18
Country Hams, 33
Cox, Maureen, 32
Cox, Tony, 35
Cream, 39
"Cry for a Shadow," 40, 44
Crystals, 41

D

"Da Do Ron Ron," 41
Dark Horse, 30
Davis, Carl, 18
"Day in the Life, A," 42
Day in the Life, A (film), 106
"Day Tripper," 60
Decca Sessions, The, 79
Derry and the Seniors, 39
Dr. John, 26
Donegan, Lonnie, 10, 18
"Don't Let Me Down," 71
Don't Let Me Down (film), 106
Double Fantasy, 14
Dowlding, William J., 42
"Do You Want to Know a Secret?" 54, 88
Drug use, 12–13, 14
Dylan, Bob, 12, 22

E

Early Beatles, The, 58
East Coast Invasion!, 85

Eastman, Heather, 32
Eastman, Lee, 37, 38
Eastman, Linda. *See* McCartney, Linda
Ed Sullivan Show, The, 10
"Eight Days a Week," 60
"Eleanor Rigby," 12, 42, 64
Electronic Sounds, 12, 22
Epstein, Brian, 18, 30, 31, 38, 39, 41
  biography, 37
  death of, 13
  first meeting with Beatles, 10
Evans, Mal, 26, 30, 37, 38
Everett, Kenny, 40
Evita (play), 39

F

Fame, Georgie, 31
Family members, 32–35
Fascher, Horst, 36
Fifth Beatles, 30–31
"Fixing a Hole," 38
Flowers in the Dirt, 18
Fluxus group, 35
"Fool on the Hill, The," 89
"For You Blue," 73
4 By the Beatles, songs on, 56, 61
Friends and lovers, 36
From Britain . . . with Beat, 85
"From Me to You," 48
Fury, Billy, 30

G

Gentle, Johnny, 30, 31
Georgie Fame's Blue Flames, 31
German-language sales pitch for shoes, 87
Gerry and the Pacemakers, 37
Get Back, 40, 41
"Get Back," 71
Give My Regards to Broad Street (movie), 32
"Give Peace a Chance," 42
Golden Beatles, The, 86
"Goodbye," 89
"Got My Mind Set on You," 22
Grade, Lew, 38
Grant, Jimmy, 40
Graves, Harry, 32, 35
Grease (movie), 39
Guinness Book of World Records, 18

H

Handmade Films, 22
"Hard Day's Night, A," 14, 55

Hard Day's Night, A (movie), 12, 26, 32, 41, 102
soundtrack, 51, 57
Hard Day's Night, A (video), 108–9
Harrison, Dhani, 32
Harrison, George
biography, 22
joins Quarry Men, 10
joins Rebels, 10
Harrison, Harold, 32
Harrison, Louise, 32
Harrison, Peter, 32
Harry, Bill, 31
Hear the Beatles Tell All, 84
Hello Goodbye (film), 106
"Hello Goodbye," 38, 66
"Hello Little Girl," 37, 41, 87
Helm, Levon, 26
"Help!" 14, 60
Help! (movie), 12, 26, 38, 41, 104
soundtrack, 59
Hendrix, Jimi, 39
Henebery, Terry, 40
"Here, There, and Everywhere," 36
Here, There, and Everywhere, 85
"Here Comes the Sun," 22
"Hey Jude," 18, 33, 69
Hey Jude, songs on, 72
"Hippy Hippy Shake," 39
Holly, Buddy, 10
Huntley, Ted, 37, 38
Hutchinson, Johnny, 31

I
"I'm a Loser," 14
"I Am the Walrus," 14, 66, 89
I Apologize, 86
Icarus, 41
Ichianagi, Toshi, 35
"I'll Cry Instead," 55
"I Don't Want to Spoil the Party," 60
"I'm Down," 60
"I Feel Fine," 55
"If I Fell," 55, 60
"If You Love Me, Baby," 44, 54
"I'll Get You," 48, 54
"I'm Happy Just to Dance with You," 55, 81
Imagine, 41
Imagine: John Lennon (movie), 33
"In My Life," 41, 42
"Inner Light, The," 69
"In Spite of All Danger," 87
"Instant Karma," 41
Interviews with Pete Best, 86
"I Saw Her Standing There," 42, 53
"I Should Have Known Better," 55
"I Want to Hold Your Hand," 39, 48, 53

"I Want You (She's So Heavy)," 14

J
James, Dick, 37, 38
Janice the Stripper, 31
Jesus Christ Superstar (play), 39
Jim Mac Band, 33
John Lennon/Plastic Ono Band, 41
Johns, Glyn, 40
Jones, Casey, 39

K
Kaempfert, Bert, 31, 40
Kirchherr, Astrid, 31, 36
Klein, Allen, 13, 18, 37, 38
Knebworth, 18
"Komm, Gib Mir Deine Hand," 54
Koschmeider, Bruno, 31, 39, 40

L
"Lady Madonna," 69
Lady Madonna (film), 106
"Layla," 32
Leadbelly (Huddie Ledbetter), 10
Lennon, Alfred, 32
Lennon, Cynthia, 33
Lennon, John
biography, 14
first band, 10
Lennon, John Charles Julian, 33
Lennon, Julia, 14, 32, 33
Lennon, Sean Taro, 14, 33
Les Stuart Quartet, 30
Lester, Richard, 32
"Let It Be," 34, 73
Let It Be, 13, 18, 30, 31, 32, 36, 40, 41
Let It Be (movie), 37, 38, 106
soundtrack, 72
Let It Be (video), 109
Life of Brian (movie), 22
"Like Dreamers Do," 37, 41, 87
Live! At The Star-Club in Hamburg, songs on, 74
Live Peace in Toronto, 30
Living in the Material World, 38, 41
"Long, Long, Long," 22
"Long and Winding Road, The," 41, 73, 89
Long Tall Sally, songs on, 56
"Love Me Do," 37, 38, 45, 54, 81
"Love of the Loved," 37, 41
Love You Make, The (Brown), 37, 38
LSD, 12–13

"Lucy in the Sky with Diamonds," 33
Lynne, Jeff, 22

M
McCabe, Peter, 38
McCartney, James, 33
McCartney, James Louis, 32
McCartney, Linda (née Eastman), 32, 37
influence on group, 13
McCartney, Mary Patricia Mohin, 32, 34
McCartney, Michael, 33, 34
McCartney, Paul
biography, 18
joins Quarry Men, 10
lawsuit by, 13
McCartney, Stella, 32
McGear, Mike. *See* McCartney, Michael
McKinnon, Duncan, 30
Maciunas, George, 35
Magic Alex. *See* Mardas, Alexis
Magical Mystery Tour, 41, 89
songs on, 65, 67
Magical Mystery Tour (movie), 13, 18, 38, 104–5
Magical Mystery Tour (video), 109
Magic Christian, The (movie), 26
Maharishi Mehesh Yogi, 12–13, 32, 36
Mamas and the Papas, 39
Man Who Gave the Beatles Away, The (Williams), 39
Mardas, Alexis, 36
Marijuana, 12
Martin, George, 10, 30, 31, 36, 37, 38, 39
biography, 40–41
Masked Melody Makers, 33
"Matchbox," 55
"Maxwell's Silver Hammer," 18, 38
MBE award, 12
Meditation, 22, 32, 36
Meet the Beatles!, songs on, 50
Merseybeat, 10, 26
Montez, Chris, 94–95
Monty Python, 22
Moody Blues, 39
Moore, Roger, 32
Moore, Tommy, 31
Movie Mania!, 85
"My Bonnie (Lies Over the Ocean)," 31, 40, 44, 45

N
Nichol, Jimmy, 31
"Nobody's Child," 22, 44

Nobody's Child: Romanian Angel Appeal, 22, 26
No One's Gonna Change Our World, 71
"Norwegian Wood," 22
Not a Second Time, 85
"Nowhere Man," 64
Nowhere Man, songs on, 64

O
"Ob-La-Di, Ob-La-Da," 18
Off the Beatle Track, 41
"Oh My My," 26
"Old Brown Shoe," 71
Old Wave, 26
"One and One Is Two," 88
Only the Beatles . . ., 79
Ono, Kyoto, 35
Ono, Yoko, 12, 14, 32, 33
biography, 34–35
influence on group, 13
"Open End Interview with The Beatles," 84
Orbison, Roy, 22, 41

P
"P.S. I Love You," 31, 45, 54, 81
Paik, Nam June, 35
"Paperback Writer," 64
Parlophone (record label), contract with, 10
Parnes, Larry, 30
Past Masters Volume One, songs on, 79
Past Masters Volume Two, songs on, 80
Paul's Christmas Album, 88
Paul Winter Consort, 41
"Penny Lane," 18, 66
Penny Lane (film), 106, 107
Perkins, Carl, 10
Pete Best Four, 30
Peter Pan (play), 36
Petty, Tom, 22
"Photograph," 26
"Piggies," 22, 42
Pilbeam, Peter, 40
Plastic Ono Band, 36
"Please Please Me," 38, 41, 48
Please Please Me, songs on, 46
Poole, Brian, 41
Powell, Cynthia, 35
Presley, Elvis, 39
Preston, Billy, 26, 30, 31
Princess Daisy (movie), 26
Producers, 40-41

Q
Quarry Men, 10, 22, 30, 31

R

Raga rock, 22
"Rain," 64
Rarities, songs on, 76, 77
Raw Energy, 79
Ready Steady Go! (video), 108
Rebels (band), 10
Reunion speculation, 13
"Revolution," 69
"Revolution 9," 12, 14, 42, 89
Revolver, 12, 22, 36, 41
  songs on, 63
Righteous Brothers, 41
Ringo (album), 26
"Ringo I Love You," 41
"River Deep, Mountain High," 41
"Robin Hood," 38
Roe, Tommy, 94–95
Rolling Stones, 38
Ronnie the Hood, 31
Rory Storm and the Hurricanes,
  26, 31
Rotogravure, 30
'Round the World, 85
Rowe, Dick, 39, 41
Royal Liverpool Philharmonic
  Orchestra, 18
Rubber Soul, 12
  songs on, 59

S

"Saints, The," 40, 44, 45
"Salute to Sir Lew Grade, A" (TV
  show), 38
Saturday Night Fever (movie), 39
"Savoy Truffle," 22
Schonfeld, Robert, 38
"Seaside Woman," 32
Sellers, Peter, 26, 41
*Sgt. Pepper's Lonely Hearts Club
  Band*, 12, 18, 22, 31, 38,
  41
  songs on, 65
Sextette (movie), 26
Shapiro, Helen, 94
"She's a Woman," 55
"She Loves You," 48
Sheridan, Tony, 10, 22, 31, 39,
  40
"Sie Leibt Dich," 54
Silver Beatles (early band name),
  10
Skiffle, 10, 26
"Slow Down," 55
Smith, Mike, 39, 41
Smith, Mimi Stanley, 35
"Some Other Guy," 88
"Something," 22, 71
Something (film), 106
Something New, songs on, 52
Some Time in New York City, 41
Songwriting credits, 42
Souvenir of Their Visit to America,
  songs on, 56
Spector, Phil, 40, 41

Spoken-word releases, 84–86
Spy Who Loved Me (movie), 32
Starkey, Elsie, 35
Starkey, Lee, 32
Starkey, Richard. *See* Starr,
  Ringo
Starkey, Zak, 35
Starr, Jason, 32
Starr, Ringo
  biography, 26
  joins Beatles, 10
  on Pete Best's drumming, 30
Steele, Tommy, 41
Stewart, Les, 30
Stigwood, Robert, 39
Storm, Rory, 26
"Strangers in the Night," 40
"Strawberry Fields Forever," 41,
  66
Strawberry Fields Forever (film),
  106
"Sue Me Sue You Blues," 38
Sullivan, Ed, 39
"Summertime," 87
Sutcliffe, John, 31
Sutcliffe, Stuart, 10, 18, 31, 36
Suzy and the Red Stripes, 32
"Sweet Georgia Brown," 44

T

Talk Downunder, 86
Taylor, Alistair, 39
Taylor, Derek, 39
Teddy Boys, 22
"Tell Me Why," 60
"Thank You Girl," 48, 54
Thank Your Lucky Stars (TV
  show), 38
"That'll Be the Day," 87
That'll Be the Day (movie), 26
"That's My Life (My Home and
  My Love)," 32
"There's a Place," 53
"Things We Said Today," 55
Things We Said Today, 85
"This Boy," 48
"This Song," 38
"Ticket to Ride," 60
"To Know Him Is To Love Him,"
  41
"Tomorrow Never Knows," 12, 14
Tours, 93
  Europe, 99
  Far East, 100
  France, 96
  Germany, 100
  Hamburg, 93–94
  with Helen Shapiro, 94
  Scotland, 93, 94, 95
  Sweden, 95
  with Tommy Roe and Chris
    Montez, 94–95
  United Kingdom, 95, 96,
    98–100

United States, 96-98, 99,
  100–101
  world, 97
Transcendental meditation, 22,
  32, 36
Traveling Wilburys, The, 22
Turner, Ike, 41
Turner, Tina, 41
"12-Bar Original," 88
"Twist and Shout," 53
Twist and Shout, songs on, 48
Twist of Lennon, A (Powell), 35

U

Una Sensazionale, 84
*Unfinished Music No. 1: Two
  Virgins*, 12, 35

V

"Valotte," 33
Vaughn, Ivan, 31
Vietnam War, 13, 14
Vincent, Gene, 14, 39
Vinton, Bobby, 38
Voorman, Klaus, 36

W

"Walking in the Park with Eloise,"
  33
Walsh, Joe, 26
Walters, Lu, 31
"We Can Work It Out," 60

West Coast Invasion!, 85
"What Goes On?" 64
"While My Guitar Gently Weeps,"
  22, 30
White, Andy, 31
White Album, 12, 22, 26, 30,
  32, 36
  songs on, 68
"Why," 44
Williams, Allan, 31, 39
Wilson, Harold, 12
Wings, 18, 30
"With a Little Help From My
  Friends," 26
"Within You, Without You," 22
With the Beatles, 36
  songs on, 47
Wonderwall (film score), 22
Wonderwall Music, 36
Wooler, Bob, 14, 39

Y

Ya-Ya, 46
"Yellow Submarine," 64
Yellow Submarine, 12, 41
Yellow Submarine (movie), 105
  soundtrack, 70
Yellow Submarine (video), 109
"Yes It Is," 60, 88
"Yesterday," 60, 88
Yesterday, songs on, 64
"You Can't Do That," 53
"You Know My Name (Look Up
  the Number)," 73
"You've Lost That Lovin' Feelin',"
  41
Young, LaMonte, 35
"You're Sixteen," 26

Photo Credits

Syndication International: 2, 9, 10, 11b, 11c, 12a, 12b, 14, 15a, 15b, 15c, 16, 17a, 18, 19a, 19c, 20b, 21, 22, 22d, 23b, 24b, 26, 27a, 27b, 28, 29a, 29b, 32a, 32b, 32c, 33, 34, 35a, 35b, 36a, 36b, 38, 49, 57, 58, 67, 69, 90, 91b, 91c, 94, 95, 96a, 96b, 97, 98, 100, 102, 103b, 104, 106, 107, 109, 111a, 111b

Photoworld/FPG International: 17b, 19b, 24a, 27c, 39a, 43b, 99, 103c, 110, 111c

Archive Photo: 30, 31

Apple Corps: 38, 39b, 40, 46, 47, 51a, 52, 59a, 59b, 63a, 65a, 65b, 70a, 70b, 72b

Dezo Hoffman/Apple Corps: 37

AP/Wide World: 6, 11a, 30a, 42

Christopher Bain: 80

United Artists: 20a, 25